Paris Insights

An Anthology

Paris Insights
An Anthology

Tom Reeves

Discover Paris!™
5816 Creek Valley Road
Edina, MN 55439-1212

Tel/fax: 212-658-9351

www.discoverparis.net
info@discoverparis.net

ISBN: 978-0-9815292-4-0

To my wife,
Monique Y. Wells,
whose efforts and support have been instrumental
in the conceptualization and creation of the project,
and whose unflagging determination has helped
bring it to its successful conclusion.

Acknowledgments

Discover Paris!™ gratefully acknowledges Melanie Moss for contributing "Prendre un Café, Prendre un Verre" as a feature article for our monthly newsletter, and for granting permission to publish the article in this anthology.

Table of Contents

Foreword: xi
Tourist or Traveler? (2002): xi

Preface: xiii

La Vie Parisienne
Les Champs-Elysées, Quintessential Paris (2000): 1
Paris-by-the-Beach (2002): 3
A Dog's Life, A Good Life: (2006) 5
River Renaissance (2004): 9
Exploring the New Drugstore (2004): 13
Hammam, Anyone? (2001): 17
Prendre un Café, Prendre un Verre or How to Be a Young Parisian (2007): 19
A Very Merry Paris Christmas! (2000): 23

Americans in Paris
Hemingway's Paris (2003): 29
Copying the Masters (2006): 31
Sylvia Beach (2004): 35
Photographing *The Da Vinci Code* (2005): 37
Homage to Man Ray (2006): 41
Wining and Dining with Juan Sánchez (2006): 45

Churches and Cathedrals
East Meets West at Notre-Dame Cathedral (2005): 53
Christian Churches in Paris (2003): 57
The Church of Val-de-Grâce (2007): 61
Saint-Sulpice (2006): 67
The King's Church (2007): 71

Tasty Treats

Dining In Paris (2001): 77
A Taste of Honey (2003): 79
Teatime in Paris (2003): 83
Summer Strawberries (2004): 87
The Macaron—A Mouthful of Heaven (2001): 91
Warming the Heart with Hot Chocolate (2005): 95
Fresh-Roasted Coffee in Paris (2007): 99
Wine Pairing for Your Christmas Feast (2004): 103

Paris, Past and Present

Vélib' (2007): 109
La Fontaine des Innocents (2007): 111
The Fearsome Dragon of the Jardin des Plantes (2007): 113
La Guillotine (2007): 115
Toni Morrison at the Louvre (2007): 117
Oldest Street Sign (2007): 119

About Discover Paris!™: 123

Index: 125

Photos and Credits: 134

Foreword

I wrote this article years ago. It expresses my vision of who Discover Paris!™ clients are—*travelers* who are looking for a little something extra when they venture beyond the home front.

Monique Y. Wells
Co-owner, Discover Paris!™

Tourist or Traveler?
(2002)

When you vacation, do you go as a tourist or as a traveler? I daresay that most people have never asked themselves the question. But for me, there is a definite distinction between the two. When one considers travel as a possible means of bridging cultural gaps in our shrinking global village, the nuances behind these words become important. And in this post-September 11 world, the distinction takes on a new significance.

Webster's Third New International Dictionary defines a tourist as "one that makes a tour," where "tour" is defined as "a journey where one returns to the starting point." It defines a traveler as "one that goes on a trip or journey... specifically, one that travels to distant or unfamiliar places." These definitions have very different connotations for me. The emphasis in the definition of "tourist" is on the return to the origin, the return home. The emphasis in the definition of "traveler" is on the going, the venturing to a new or foreign place.

In my opinion (based on years of observing visitors to my adopted home, Paris), tourists are more likely to maintain a distance between themselves and the places that they visit. Their purpose in traveling is to "see the sights," take photos and have their photos taken in front of said sights, and perhaps even tempt fate by eating a local dish or two. They often travel in tour groups, which offer the advantage of obtaining cursory information about the sights visited, but also have the disadvantage of discouraging individual discovery. Thus, at travel destinations tourists behave as one would before department-store window displays, viewing them but not venturing into the store to browse or to buy.

In contrast, travelers interact much more with the people and places found at their travel destinations. They enjoy not only the main sights, but also the back streets and hidden neighborhoods in and around their destinations. They seek out the things that differentiate the places visited from their home territory. They observe the local culture and inhabitants, and seek to understand them. And in the process, they share information about their own culture.

When I first visited Paris at the age of twenty-eight, I was strictly in tourist mode. I traveled with several friends—we met in London and spent three days there before moving on to the City of Light. We spent three days in Paris as well. While there, we partook of all the standard tourist activities—we rode the *bateaux mouches*, visited the Latin Quarter, climbed up to the gallery of Notre-Dame—I have plenty of photos to show for the trip. I then reluctantly parted from the group and made my way back to the States, while the rest of my friends went on to Amsterdam.

One thing struck me upon our arrival in Paris, the impact of which did not hit me until much later. As we exited the metro stop Cadet and dragged our bags through the 9th *arrondissement* looking for our hotel, I noticed that the people on the streets did not look like what I considered a French person to be. They were Arabs, or more precisely, North Africans. And they were everywhere! I vaguely wondered why they were there, but immediately became caught up in keeping up with my friends and trying to find the hotel.

I always had an interest in the French language, and was thrilled to visit the birthplace of the tongue that had for so long been music to my ears. At that time, France represented a language for me, not a people. Certainly not a mix of peoples! And three days is not enough time to grasp much in the way of culture if you are not looking for it.

My visit fueled my fantasy of moving to a French-speaking country, but my sense of Paris' cultural diversity was not yet awakened. It was only after I actively sought a job in France that I began to learn more about the history and culture of the country. I remembered our trek through the 9th *arrondissement*, and began to realize that France's population is every bit as diverse as that of the United States.

So when I moved to France, I did so as a traveler. Not only was I determined to learn about the various peoples who reside there, why they came and how they live, but I also made up my mind to visit other countries with the same perspective. As a result, my voyages have been much fuller and richer, and my understanding and appreciation of my own American culture has deepened.

What is the moral of my story? Be a traveler, not a tourist. I think you'll appreciate the difference!

Preface

Tom Reeves

For eight years, Discover Paris!™ has lovingly and faithfully prepared its monthly newsletter, *Paris Insights*, for its clients. Our publication has steadily evolved, becoming longer and more informative over the years as we became increasingly committed to providing our readers with information that they could not find on "just any old Web site."

Because we would like to share some of our favorite and most popular newsletters with a larger public, we bring you this anthology. We have adorned it with numerous photos that not only illustrate the newsletter topics, but also provide you with our artistic sense of what the City of Light is all about.

With the exception of minor edits, the newsletters have been reproduced as they were published. The year of publication is indicated beneath each title. Where updates are relevant (for example, businesses that have closed or moved), a notation is made in *italics* at the end of the newsletter.

We hope that you will enjoy this anthology!

Tom Reeves
President, Discover Paris!™

La Vie Parisienne

Les Champs-Elysées, Quintessential Paris

(2000)

On a rare sunny day in early spring, my colleague and I decided to take a ride on "La Roue de Paris," the huge Ferris wheel that sits at the end of the Tuileries garden at Place de la Concorde. Roughly sixty meters (197 feet) in height, it was the star attraction of the twenty-one wheels erected on the Champs-Elysées for Paris' millennium celebration. There were a few concession stands at the base of the wheel, and the lovely aroma of golden-brown *gaufres* (Belgian waffles) permeated the air.

The view of Paris from the wheel was breathtaking, particularly on this clear day. The wooded mound of Butte Chaumont and the chalk-white splendor of Sacré-Cœur were in the distance, and much closer, the dome at Invalides looked as though you could reach out and touch it. The precision of the Tuileries garden with its first spring blossoms lay at our feet, and it was marvelous to be able to see this landscape in its entirety. But for me, the most impressive view from the wheel was that of the Champs-Elysées, the world's grandest avenue.

Between the obelisk at Place de la Concorde and the Arc de Triomphe lies the 330-year-old thoroughfare that is renowned everywhere. In the distance farther to the west lies the Grande Arche de la Défense. Built under François Mitterand, the monument completes the line of grandeur that begins with the Louvre and the Tuileries garden. Postcards simply cannot capture the power and the spirit that emanate from this magnificent example of city planning.

The Champs-Elysées was born in 1670 as the result of Le Nôtre's design of a landscaped garden beyond the Jardin des Tuileries, and the lining of its promenade between the Louvre and the hill called Chaillot (now the site of the Arc de Triomphe) with trees. During the 1700s, when the only road in the area was what is now rue du Faubourg Saint-Honoré, magnificent *hôtels particuliers* (mansions) were built on this street with individual gardens designed to overlook the Champs-Elysées.

Though it was a haven for criminals by night for more than a century, constant remodeling and upgrading turned the Champs-Elysées into a veritable playground during the day. Circuses, concerts, and other types of performances for public amusement flourished. Many of the pavilions and theaters that housed these activities are still found in the gardens on either side of the first stretch of the avenue between Place de la Concorde and the Rond-Point. The pavilions are occupied by some of Paris' most chic restaurants, and several of the theaters are still operational.

The installation of public lighting on the avenue occurred in 1840, and later, the efforts of Napoleon III finally made it a safe place at night. Many fine residences were built along the Champs-Elysées to rival those on rue du Faubourg Saint-Honoré. Thomas Jefferson occupied one of these residences from 1785–89, when he was the US ambassador to France. Interestingly, several of these *hôtels particuliers* were inhabited by courtesans, or mistresses, of wealthy men.

Once you venture past the Rond-Point, the landscape changes from peaceful and picturesque to glitzy and ultracommercial. Big business is pervasive, with banks, airline companies, and anonymous corporate offices lining the street. Movie theaters, shopping arcades, and perfume and clothing boutiques jostle with sidewalk cafés and fast-food restaurants to compete for the crowds that descend upon the avenue daily (roughly 300,000 people on an average day!). Evenings and weekends are even more bustling, with business activities yielding to leisure pursuits such as night-clubbing and people-watching.

The Arc de Triomphe was mounted at the far end on the Chaillot hill, which had been lowered by five meters between 1768 and 1774 by the engineer Jean-Rodolphe Perronet. Conceived as a tribute to the French military, this is where the Tomb of the Unknown Soldier from World War I lies, as well as the Flame of Remembrance that was first ignited on Armistice Day in 1923. Military processions have made a tradition of marching past the arch as a powerful symbol of victory. The Prussians and the Nazis had their turn during the Franco-Prussian War and the Occupation of Paris, but France and its allies also marched victorious after World War I and during the Liberation of Paris near the end of World War II.

Public celebrations and rallies have been a part of the history of the avenue for centuries, and that tradition still holds today. During the May 1968 crisis instigated by the student revolt in Paris, a demonstration of support for Charles de Gaulle was held on the Champs-Elysées. Every year, the Tour de France terminates on the "Champs" (the French are avid cycling fans), and thousands of people cram the sidewalks to cheer on their favorite team. And what would Paris be without its annual Bastille Day celebration, including a huge parade on the avenue with a fabulous aeronautical display overhead and fireworks once dusk falls?

Whether you go to get a glimpse of the romance of centuries past, to do some serious shopping, or to idle away the hours at a sidewalk café, the Champs-Elysées is a "must-do" for everyone!

Paris-by-the-Beach
(2002)

Welcome to Paris-by-the-Beach! Three kilometers (1.8 miles) of riverfront highway in the heart of Paris have been transformed into a resort strand, complete with beach volleyball, palm trees, and ice-cream stands. Creating a beach in the center of Paris has required the transport of 18,000 cubic meters (24,000 cubic yards) of sand, eighty palm trees, 150 beach umbrellas, twenty-two changing rooms, 150 decorative banners, four snack bars, and various other items, all supported by a $1.5 million budget that is being paid for by the city of Paris. Let the summer fun begin!

July 21 marked the opening of Paris Plage, as it is officially called, and it attracted hundreds of sunbathers who bared their bodies on stretches of grass or sand along the river. Thousands more strolled along the riverfront highway that runs parallel to the new beaches.

But not everybody was on foot: roller-bladers, bicyclists, and babies pushed in strollers mixed with the crowd. Several bridges, including the Pont des Arts, Pont Neuf, and the Pont au Change, were lined with spectators who chose to survey the beach scene from above rather than descend to the crowded riverfront below. The day was sunny and warm, which boded well for the popularity of the ersatz beach that has captured the imagination of Parisians.

Large fluorescent yellow signs are positioned at intervals along the quays. These provide practical information about the activities planned over the four-week period during which the beach will be open, including concerts, art exhibits, dance performances, and sporting events. Even street art is being encouraged: on opening day we saw artists using spray paint to create a graffiti mural stretching a hundred meters along the riverbank.

Here is a brief overview of the activities:
- Music: rhythm and blues, techno, classical, Armenian, accordion, fanfare.
- Sports: rock climbing, golf, roller-blading, *pétanque* (a type of bowling played on the sand), beach volleyball, fishing.

- Various other events: clowns, juggling, dance, and, of course, sunbathing.

Several thousand people had visited Paris Plage by the time that an Armenian band played lively music on Monday evening, July 29, to a crowd of enthusiastic spectators. Farther along the quay, *pétanque* players were concentrating on their games on the sandy stretch set aside for them. Across the Seine, people gathered on the riverbank to listen to the music, while the familiar *bateaux mouches* (riverboats) plied by. It was a peaceful scene, and the setting sun presented a picture-postcard photo opportunity for the scores of Parisians and visitors promenading on the sidewalks and quays.

The fun ends on August 18, when the city rolls up the beach and reopens the riverfront highway to commuters returning from vacation. In the meantime, visitors to Paris this summer will enjoy this unique opportunity to stroll along the transformed riverbank.

଼ଠ   ଔଃ

Parisians have enjoyed Paris Plage every year since 2002.

A Dog's Life, A Good Life
(2006)

Dogs are abundant in Paris. We see them strolling with their masters—sometimes tugging at their leashes in directions that the masters do not want to go, other times plodding peacefully ahead, unperturbed by their surroundings. Often, we see an owner with two dogs, one on a lead and one walking free. (We find ourselves wondering if the dogs take turns walking free, or rather if the one on the leash is less well behaved and is always so confined.) We see them tied up at the door of the bakery or the grocery store, lying at the feet of their master at the neighborhood café or bar, or posing as a shaggy barrier over which one must step to cross the threshold of a store owner's boutique. Jack Russell terriers are very popular, as are bichons and other small dogs, but one sees a good number of Labrador retrievers and other large breeds as well.

The average dog on the streets of Paris appears well groomed and well trained. It frequently enjoys the company of other dogs on sidewalks, in public squares, and in parks and gardens. It is virtually never unaccompanied, and even when allowed off its leash it is generally not found too distant from its owner. Visitors often marvel at the comportment of these canines, which make up part of the Paris *mystique*.

What kinds of relationships do Parisians have with their dogs? We determined to interview three dog owners to find out.

Jane is an American who has been living in Paris for twenty-six years. She currently resides in a fourth-floor apartment located in Les Halles quarter. Her dog, Rita, a cross between a poodle and Tibetan terrier, is an extremely affectionate creature. Rita barks her greeting from behind the apartment door long before Jane's guests reach her landing, and rises up on her hind legs and eagerly paws the air to greet any guests who enter.

Jane told us that the human resource officer of the company she worked for advised her to get a dog to serve as a companion (*animal de companie*) for her retirement years. At that time (five years ago), the company was laying off employees who were nearing retirement age.

Taking this advice, Jane began visiting the humane society, talking to dog

Rita

Matisse

Jimpy

breeders and looking in pet stores. She determined that the dogs at the humane society were too old to adopt, and that the purebred dogs at the breeders were too expensive. She found three-month-old Rita, a crossbreed from a farm in Brittany, at a pet store along the quay that lies on the Seine between Châtelet and Pont Neuf.

Jane was pleased that Rita, though blessed with a calm personality, would bark if a stranger walked down the hallway of the apartment. Jane learned that once Rita could determine that the person in the hallway was not a stranger (by smell or by the footfall?), she would not bark.

Jane takes Rita out for a walk at least three times a day. In the morning, Rita accompanies her mistress when Jane buys her newspaper and goes to a café for breakfast. Around noon, Jane goes to a restaurant and runs errands. Again, Rita accompanies her. In the evening, Jane takes Rita for a stroll around the neighborhood.

Parisians are famous for having their dogs accompany them into restaurants, and Jane and Rita greatly enjoy this privilege. In one restaurant where Rita is known, the waiter brings her a bowl of water and a slice of salami (as well as a slice for Jane). After Jane settles in, Rita makes her rounds under the table (restrained by a leash) to look for scraps of food, then sits calmly while Jane dines.

Jane and Rita's experience at Starbucks, however, was an entirely different matter. Jane told us how she and Rita investigated the first Starbucks café when it opened in Paris. Because she is from Seattle, where Starbucks was founded, she thought she would have an affinity for this coffee shop. But when she walked in with Rita, she was told that she could not bring the dog in. Jane raised a fuss, but to no avail. Three elderly French ladies behind her (with no dogs) said, "Are they asking you to leave because of your cute little doggie?" When Jane replied in the affirmative they said,

"Humpf! Then we are leaving, too!" And they marched out right behind her.

Giovanna is an Italian woman who, with her French husband, creates hand-painted porcelain in a studio near rue Mouffetard. Her dog, Matisse, is a *teckel à poil dur* (wirehaired dachshund).

Giovanna told us that she has owned dogs since an early age. The first was given to her at the age of nine, when she woke up in the hospital after an operation to find it under her bed. (At that time hospital rules in Italy were not as strict as they are today.) She lost the dog when she was twelve years old; it did not come back one night and she found out the next day that it had been hit by a car. Giovanna recounts, "Once you lose a dog you are sad and don't want to go through that again."

She purchased her next dog at the age of eighteen, when she was studying in Paris. One day she was looking at puppies in the pet shops along the quay. One jumped out of its cage and clung to her sweater. It was a match made in heaven! Sadly, the dog died twelve years later of *maladie de Carré* (distemper). It went mad and, Giovanna believes, suffered so much that it "committed suicide" by jumping out of a fourth-floor window.

Giovanna purchased Matisse from a dog breeder for her son, who is now fourteen years old. When Giovanna goes on vacation she has two solutions for caring for the dog. The first is to leave Matisse with the breeder, where it is cared for in familiar surroundings. The second is to choose the friends with whom she goes on vacation carefully, to be sure that they and the dogs they bring with them are compatible. Often Giovanna goes on a holiday with a friend who has a West Island terrier with which Matisse can play.

Matisse loves to go to the country for vacation, where he runs and has total freedom.

For strolling in Paris, Giovanna takes Matisse once a day to his favorite place—the Jardin du Luxembourg. The park has lots of trees for him to sniff, and has a special place for owners to walk their dogs. It is also equipped with a dispenser that provides plastic gloves for the owners to pick up the excrement their dogs leave behind.

Olivier hails from Reunion Island, a French overseas department located in the Indian Ocean east of Madagascar. He often walks his dog, Jimpy, a whippet, without a lead. Olivier explained that while the city of Paris requires dog owners to use a leash, his dog is well behaved and always comes to him when called. Indeed, Olivier carries a leash with him, and uses it whenever he takes Jimpy to the nearby park Butte Chaumont. There he lets Jimpy run and smell the grass until the park cop blows his whistle, at which time he attaches the leash.

Jimpy belongs to Olivier's girlfriend Jennifer. When Olivier first met Jennifer four years ago, he was concerned about the dog. In Reunion, everyone has a garden

Olivier and Jimpy

where dogs can play. He thought, *The dog isn't going to be happy [in the city].* However, Jimpy made Olivier change his mind very quickly. The dog goes everywhere with Olivier, even in the metro.

Olivier always takes a dog carrier with him. When they are in the metro, Jimpy stands patiently on the quay with Olivier until the train arrives. When they board the train, Jimpy jumps into the bag and remains there until time to get off. Without the bag, Jimpy would be fidgety, as her body is sensitive to hard surfaces.

Olivier and Jennifer take Jimpy into restaurants all the time. Sometimes they get refused, especially in Thai restaurants. When this happens, Olivier tries to convince the owner that the dog is very special. When she is admitted, Jimpy stays quietly in the dog bag at the foot of the table.

All three dog owners whom we interviewed indicated that Parisians have a soft spot for dogs. Jane told of how salespeople in BHV department store rushed to greet Rita the day after they had reacted indifferently to Jane's presence without the dog. Giovanna recounted how once, when she went into a perfume store that had a strong odor, a saleslady offered to take the dog outside and watch it while she shopped. And Olivier noted that when Jimpy is with him people smile and talk to him.

Jane, Giovanna, and Olivier have a strong affection and a sense of responsibility toward their dogs. These are but three among some 200,000 dogs in Paris. They provide their owners with lasting and faithful companionship.

There will always be Paris and Parisians will always have their dogs!

River Renaissance
(2004)

Mention the word "river" in relation to Paris, and people inevitably think of the Seine. Few know about the Bièvre, another river that played an important role in the history of the city.

The Bièvre begins its course in Guyancourt (Les Yvelines), meanders through southern suburbs, and runs through the 13th and 5th *arrondissements* (districts) of Paris before emptying into the Seine near the Gare d'Austerlitz. For five centuries, it was polluted by waste from factories and artisanal workshops in Paris and its environs, and was finally enclosed over a long section of its course. Roughly eight kilometers of the river currently run underground in Paris.

A project is now underway to uncover several kilometers of the Bièvre by the year 2007. A coalition of thirty-five associations, committees, school organizations, and syndicates are working together to make this happen. And as part of the campaign to raise awareness of their efforts, coalition members are sponsoring annual cultural events. One of the most interesting of these members is Lezarts de la Bièvre, an association that promotes contemporary artists whose studios are located in the vicinity of the river.

Every year since 2001, Lezarts de la Bièvre has organized an open house for these artists, in hopes of inspiring the community to rediscover the traces of past life in the neighborhoods through which the river flowed. Simultaneously, the open houses provide exposure and support for area artists. The most recent event, held in June 2004, proposed visits to seventy-two ateliers and several outdoor concerts. Maps were distributed for five different areas, each with a different walking itinerary.

The most original aspect of the open house is the annual treasure hunt—an artist is selected to "decorate" buildings and walls on the route with works of art, and the general public is encouraged to search for the images. Stencil artists have been chosen since the event began in 2001, and samples of their work still punctuate the landscape of the 5th and 13th districts.

Miss Tic has adorned Paris with her images of a voluptuous woman accompanied by brief, often enigmatic phrases, for years. She was the artist selected to inaugurate

what Lezarts de la Bièvre has christened *Lezarts sur les Murs* (The Arts on the Walls). The following year, Jerôme Mesnager left his mark on several walls and windows, using a few swaths of white paint to create what looks like a stylized version of a man made only of the muscles of the human anatomy.

In 2003, a different man graced the walls of the "Bièvre Zone"—painted all in black and dressed in a trench coat and hat, he carries a briefcase (or perhaps a suitcase), but is always engaged in decidedly non-businesslike activities. Passersby find him in a hammock slung in the most interesting places, or being pulled along by a gust of wind that has caught his umbrella, or sitting in a shallow boat accompanied by bunnies and butterflies. One particularly whimsical design portrays this "Shadow Man" walking a hippo on a leash, the hippo holding a flower in its mouth.

The artist, who uses the pseudonym Nemo, has become decidedly popular. He sometimes works with Mesnager, and when he does, Parisians find the "Muscle Man" and the "Shadow Man" portrayed together in interesting poses around town.

This year, Lezarts de la Bièvre engaged Mosko et Associés to literally paint the town. The group consists of two artists, Gérard and Michel, who represent the fauna of Africa and Asia in vivid color and detail. Meerkats have appeared in the boats where Nemo's "Shadow Man" plies imaginary waters, and tigers have been seen roaming in neighborhoods previously devoid of wildlife. An elementary-school retaining wall now bears the image of a rainbow upon which tiny elephants and giraffes are walking toward an unknown destination, while beneath the arc, a large giraffe seeks to graze upon the barren ground.

Lezarts sur les Murs has provided the citizens of the 5th and 13th *arrondissements* with an impressive array of street art that bears no resemblance to the graffiti that is now ubiquitous in Paris. Many of Nemo's works have been defaced by such graffiti, though, curiously, Mesnager's and Miss Tic's works remain mostly intact. In any event, the artful treasure hunts created by Lezarts de la Bièvre are certain to bring delight to both residents and visitors to the "Bièvre Zone" for a long time to come.

◈   ◈

Rather than uncovering the Bièvre—an expensive undertaking—the city of Paris has recently marked the course of the river with medallions embedded in the sidewalk.

Bar:
Michele Saee et Bruno Pingeot, architects
P. Dhennequin, photographer

Brasserie:
Michele Saee et Bruno Pingeot, architects
P. Dhennequin, photographer

Press stand:
Michele Saee et Bruno Pingeot, architects
D. Maitre, photographer

Wine *cave*:
Michele Saee et Bruno Pingeot, architects
D. Maitre, photographer

Exploring the New Drugstore
(2004)

Paris has hundreds of pharmacies, but only one drugstore.

Like a phoenix, the Drugstore Publicis rose from the ashes of the building at 133, avenue des Champs-Elysées after it was destroyed in a conflagration in September 1972. Following the fire, Publicis founder Marcel Bleustein-Blanchet created a new, modern structure to replace the burned edifice that had housed his company and the decidedly Gallicized, upscale rendition of an American cultural icon—the drugstore.

Thirty years later, Drugstore Publicis closed for extensive remodeling. On February 5, 2004, it opened in a bolder, more contemporary structure. Iranian-born architect Michele Saee has created a temple of contemporary art, interior design, and hi-tech kitsch for the rich, the famous, and the simply curious.

The newly renovated Drugstore Publicis is home for two movie theaters, a tobacconist/international press stand, a traditional French pharmacy, two restaurants (one of them a *brasserie*), a gourmet food boutique, two *caves*—one for wine and one for cigars, gift shops, a cosmetics boutique, and a bookstore.

Upon entering the Drugstore from the Champs-Elysées, one encounters a tobacco shop with a press stand, and the undulating curves of the glass partition of the *brasserie* Publicis. The Drugstore's blue-gray walls immediately plunge the visitor into an atmosphere of 21st-century chic, with dark hardwood floors and a spattering of neon above and around the bar of the *brasserie.*

To the left, the *brasserie's* voluminous bubble-like extension onto the sidewalk of the Champs-Elysées provides space for a café setting. In contrast, the interior is dusky and intimate. There is an area at the back of the restaurant that was initially reserved for nonsmokers only during lunch and dinner. But due to popular demand, nonsmokers who wish to frequent the restaurant during tea time (3:00 p.m. to 6:00 p.m.) can now be assured of a smoke-free environment.

The second restaurant, called Marcel, is private. Named after the Publicis founder, it has its own entrance on the Champs-Elysées. Screens over the fishbowl-like windows protect diners from public scrutiny.

Publicis Drugstore façade

Moving past the *brasserie* and press shop, spaces on the left and right are devoted to temporary exhibits. Beyond this area, the visitor encounters video art by Nam June Paik: flashing screens forming the image of a man who might represent Inspector Maigret—three screens make up his hatband, and a fourth represents one of his eyes. Passing the display of items for sale in the pharmacy, the visitor continues to the entryway of the gourmet shop.

The gourmet shop (*épicerie*) at the back of the store is operated by Alain Soulard, a *protégé* of master French chef Alain Ducasse. This emporium, which can be entered from rue Verlet, features an entire wall devoted to sandwiches, packaged organic meals, and bottled fruit juices and waters. Fresh breads are for sale adjacent to the refrigerated section. Coffees and teas, perfect pastas and vacuum-packed risottos, British oatcakes and sweet biscuits, are found among the items along another wall, and products by the up-and-coming Belgian *chocolatier* Pierre Marcolini are featured here as well.

The take-out area presents traditional savory tarts and fresh French- and Swedish-style sandwiches, but also prominently displays Iranian caviars, smoked sturgeon, Iberian ham, Japanese noodles, and wasabi. Braided salmon and sole, lobster *à l'Américaine, foie gras chaud aux pommes,* and *blanquette de lotte au chablis* are but some of the creations that Soulard proposes to the Drugstore's affluent clientele.

Gourmet fare even extends to Café Nescafé, a small espresso stand where hot and iced teas and coffees (with or without added flavorings) are sold alongside juices, *frappés,* and milkshakes. *Viennoiserie* and individually wrapped muffins can also be purchased at this counter.

The bookstore, located across from the coffee stand, offers a wide range of books. All titles are in French, with the exception of one small shelf of books labeled *Litterature V.O.,* where English-language books are available.

Walking down to the lower level, the visitor encounters a brightly lit space occupied by Shu Uemura cosmetics, prior to reaching the door of the France Inter Studio, from which José Artur's popular radio show *Le Pop Club* is now broadcast.

In a somber recess on this level, a wine boutique offers vintages from all over the world. Wines from little known wine-producing countries such as Canada, Israel, and Mexico are given equal footing with selections from well-known producers such as the United States, Australia, and Argentina. Selections are arranged in alphabetical order according to country. When the shop first opened, no French wines were available (to the amazement and chagrin of many French visitors). But Gérard Margeon, the *sommelier* in charge (yet another of Alain Ducasse's team of epicurean professionals), now showcases a selection of wines from the best of France's little-known wine producers alongside the foreign vintages. The boutique hosts a free wine tasting every Thursday evening from 6:00 p.m. to 8:00 p.m.

Adjacent to the wine boutique, a *cave à cigares* sells only stogies made in Cuba. Ramon Allones, Romeo y Julieta (Winston Churchill's favorite), and Sancho Panza are among the brands that are offered there.

An eclectic assortment of gifts is available throughout the store, on both the upper and lower levels. Some of the more interesting items present on our last visit included cufflinks by Dunhill, teddy bears by J. C. de Castelbajac (who also created the clothing that the Drugstore employees sport every day), handbags made of gazelle hide (Conde de Cerrageria), and lamps made of jars filled with *berlingots* (a popular French candy) called "Light in Food." Not to be outdone, the pharmacy offers hot water bottles emblazoned with images of Marilyn Monroe or the Union Jack. A newly installed exhibit featuring the ultimate in hi-tech gadgetry such as a wireless television screen, and pendants that display computerized photo images, can be found on the lower level. Watches from Van Cleef and Arpels and Mont Blanc are luxury items that Publicis sells alongside the hi-tech merchandise.

Publicis frequently changes the products that are displayed on its shelves, so regular visitors can always expect to find something new there. The staff is hospitable and helpful, which adds to the pleasure of perusing the store's eclectic offerings. The Drugstore is one of Paris' premier places to shop for the person who has everything!

ℬ   ℭ

As of 1 January 2008, all eating establishments in France are nonsmoking.

Hammam, Anyone?

(2001)

For a both sensual and spiritual experience in Paris, one need look no further than—a mosque?

Yes, that's correct! The complex housing the Grande Mosquée de Paris offers an authentic *hammam*, complete with steam rooms, wading pool, and massage area.

The mosque is an authentic place of worship for the Muslims of various origins who live in Paris. It was constructed in honor of the contribution of France's North African colonies during World War I, and Tunisian, Moroccan, and Algerian artisans of the day were responsible for the fine craftsmanship evident in the Islamic motifs that compose the interior design. A brief visit to the main courtyard will serve to inspire you before moving on to the baths.

The mosque also offers a *souk* (marketplace), restaurant, and tearoom in addition to the *hammam*. The entry to the *hammam*, restaurant, and tearoom is located on the corner of rue Geoffroy Saint-Hilaire and rue Daubenton. You are transported into another world and another time when you stop here for North African pastries and a glass (not a cup!) of tea. Roses and holly are among the plants that adorn the patio here. The entrance to the *hammam*, used on different days by men and women, is also accessible from the patio. It is reserved for men on Tuesdays and Sundays only; women have the lion's share of privileges, with entry allowed on Mondays, Wednesdays, Thursdays, Fridays, and Saturdays.

The entrance to this enchanting sauna is adjacent to the space that houses the pastry stand supplying the tearoom. Behind the double doors is a waiting area, after which is the entry to the actual *hammam*. Payment is made at the desk in the anteroom that opens onto an area furnished with massage tables and cushioned platforms where you can indulge in mint tea and pastry.

After soaking in the atmosphere, move on to the series of steam rooms, each hotter than the one before. The cool wading pool is found in the hottest room. After your sauna, you may choose to receive a vigorous rubdown called *gommage*, the purpose of which is to remove the dead skin cells from your newly steam-cleaned body and stimulate the microcirculation.

There is an entry fee of 85 FF, and massages cost an additional 55 FF (ten minutes) or 160 FF (thirty minutes). *Gommage* is 55 FF. You may either bring your own towel or rent one on the premises (20 FF). A swim suit is obligatory for hygienic purposes (at least the bottom of a bikini for women), but you can shed it once inside. For a fee of 200 FF or 300 FF, you are allowed entry into the *hammam*, massage for ten or thirty minutes, *gommage*, soap, and a glass of mint tea. Relaxation and refreshment await you in this oasis of culture.

La Grande Mosquée de Paris
Hammam and tearoom
39, rue Geoffroy Saint-Hilaire
75005 Paris
Tel: 01.43.38.20 or 01.43.31.18.14

Main entry of the mosque
1, rue du Puits-de-l'Ermite
75005 Paris

Prendre un Café, Prendre un Verre or How to Be a Young Parisian

(2007)

by Melanie Moss

1. Stand to the right on the escalator.
2. Place your slice of bread on the tablecloth rather than your plate.
3. Depending on the time of day, take the time to *prendre un café* (have a coffee) or *prendre un verre* (have a drink).

Behold three French customs that rival those of political stature in their significance. The third, the art of simultaneously enjoying both your beverage and the atmosphere of a café or bar, is as important to understanding the French way of life as a trip to the Louvre. Practicing this ritual breaks up a tedious day of tourism, and offers a glimpse into what makes Parisian culture tick. Parisians of all ages profit from this elemental activity, so why shouldn't you? With the suggestions listed below, young travelers in particular can exercise their independence and eagerness to participate in the periodic *verre*, all while blending in with indigenous Parisian youth.

The Breakfast Wake-up Call:
Step into the fresh air a bit earlier than you might otherwise leave your hotel, and fall into the tempo of the Parisian morning. Unless your hotel breakfast is free, it is likely to be overpriced, cloying, and lacking in the genuine taste of French products. Open your day by claiming your right to the best possible *croissant* or *pain au chocolat* (chocolate-filled pastry) you can find, stepping into whichever *boulangerie-pâtisserie* (bakery) has opened its doors, standing in line with the pre-office crowd, and subsequently savoring it at the sit-down or stand-up counter in the shop.

Alternatively, the following cafés serve great *croissants* and espresso:

Le Nemrod (6th *arrondissement*)
51, rue du Cherche-Midi
Metro: Saint-Placide or Sèvres Babylone

This *brasserie* is in constant motion. Enjoy a coffee or fruit juice on the terrace or indoors—it will give you the energy and inspiration to glance through the neighboring high-class department store, Le Bon Marché.

Au Rocher de Cancale (2nd *arrondissement*)
78, rue Montorgueil
Metro: Etienne Marcel or Sentier

Both trendy and classic at the same time, this 2nd *arrondissement* hot spot welcomes the Montorgueil quarter's hip clientele into its aged interiors. It was once the preferred dining spot of such 19th-century luminaries as Honoré de Balzac, Alexandre Dumas *père*, and Eugène Sue. Sip your espresso while watching the passersby at the lively Montorgueil market, and imagine yourself transported back to the era of these literary giants.

Tourists Merit a Cocktail:
Following a day of exploration, take a break before returning to the hotel to prepare for dinner. Enjoy a 6:00 p.m. reduced-price happy hour (the phenomenon has caught on in France) alongside a terrace full of Parisians meeting up with friends for a glassful.

Feria Café (4th *arrondissement*)
4, rue du Bourg-Tibourg
Metro: Saint Paul

As soon as the call of happy hour strikes, revelers of the Marais quarter assemble on Feria's spacious terrace located near the Pompidou museum. If the flavored martini (ask the bartender to make one with *manzana*) goes quickly to your head, indulge in tasty *tapas* from the restaurant's menu.

Indiana Bar (five locations in Paris)

You may ask why we are suggesting a bar with a stateside namesake in which to spend your limited time in the City of Light. This is a legitimate question! At each of the city's Indiana locations you will find a buzzing happy hour in a barroom stocked full of the city's natives, all gathering to enjoy the comfortable pub setting and low cocktail prices. Cold weather doesn't close down the terrace, and you will find no better spot to tune in to the melodic notes of Parisian gossip. If you crave a

pre-dinner boost, go for the *grignotages* (snacks). You will see other French youths foregoing escargots for nachos or guacamole.

Post-Dinner Enjoyment:
Your family or accompanying travelers may be heading back to the hotel, bellies full, but that doesn't mean you should miss experiencing what Paris has to offer by night. Seize on these hours, which reveal another perspective of the capital and its youth, all over a *verre* and some local music.

Le Divan du Monde (18th *arrondissement*)
75, rue des Martyrs
Metro: Pigalle

Step out of the metro to the beckoning movement of the Moulin Rouge windmill, symbolizing the streets of the Pigalle quarter, and head to the Divan for live music in a trendy concert space. Here you will glimpse a realm of the Paris that never sleeps, and enjoy the lounge's varied music program.

Le Caveau des Oubliettes (5th *arrondissement*)
52, rue Galande
Metro: Saint Michel

Something about jazz marries perfectly with Parisian culture. Perhaps the appreciation of the music is augmented by the effects of red wine, which seems to flow more abundantly than water, or the spontaneous nature of the city's people, which echoes the improvised notes of the jazz genre. These captivating elements unite in a little *cave* (cellar) a few steps away from the lively place Saint-Michel. Sip a beer in Le Caveau's ground-level pub, and then descend, with sober caution, the winding stone stairs into the Middle Ages (the *cave* dates back to the 12th century). Within these ancient walls, you will find young Parisians relishing the free, high-spirited jazz emanating from a tiny stage adjacent to the bar. Be patient, grab a seat, and realize that an experience such as this one occurs only in Paris.

With a day full of *verres* behind you, catch the last metro back to your hotel, leaving the bar a bit before 1:00 a.m. If midnight hunger happens to seize you, note that both Le Divan du Monde and Le Caveau des Oubliettes are conveniently situated near *crêpe* stands!

A Very Merry Paris Christmas!
(2000)

What is the best thing about Christmas in Paris?
Perhaps it is the combination of tradition and contemporary manifestations of this most important holiday. Because Paris is a city filled with people from provinces such as Provence and Alsace, ancient customs from these areas have become an integral part of celebrations here.

For example, Père Noël (our Santa Claus) was introduced to the Parisians around the turn of the century by department-store merchants who wished to develop a character to promote the custom of exchanging gifts at the beginning of the New Year (*les étrennes*). The character is based on the figure of Saint Nicolas, who has been celebrated at the *Foire de Saint-Nicolas* in Strasbourg since the Middle Ages. Père Noël is thinner than his American counterpart, but dresses similarly in a long red robe trimmed in white. He also has a full white beard. While he is not as omnipresent in France as he is in the US, he can be seen in front of Paris department stores such as BHV (Bazar de l'Hôtel de Ville).

The Christmas tree is also presumed to have its origins in medieval eastern France, where Christmas Eve was the occasion to remember not only the birth of Christ but also the Fall of Adam. A fir tree decorated with red apples was meant to represent the Garden of Eden, a terrestrial paradise. But it wasn't until the late 19th century that Parisians began to adapt the fir tree as a symbol of Christmas, after Alsatians, fleeing the east due to Germany's capture of the region, brought this custom with them to Paris.

Today, Christmas trees are a totally secular symbol of Christmas. They abound in Paris from about mid-November through mid-January every year. The *mairie*, or town hall, of each *arrondissement* (district) has a *sapin de Noël*, as does the Hôtel de Ville that serves all of Paris. And department stores make full use of this Christmas tradition as part of their increasingly elaborate decorations for the season (their window displays are a veritable wonderland for kids). At home, children place their shoes under the tree or next to the chimney to receive their gifts, as opposed to hanging stockings as we do in the US.

The quiet, introverted atmosphere that Paris streets had for Christmases of years past has given way to more festive displays of holiday cheer. There is no shortage of bright and gay yet elegant Christmas decorations on the major avenues and shopping thoroughfares around town. As might be expected, the Champs-Elysées takes the prize with breathtaking, innovative decor year after year. But place Vendôme, rue Saint-Honoré, and rue du Faubourg Saint-Honoré are among many other streets and *places* that hold their own quite well. The Eiffel Tower will offer an amazing spectacle this Christmas, as it is still bedecked with the sparkling lights that it donned to celebrate the millenium this year.

But more endearing than these displays are the decorations that one finds while walking through smaller commercial areas. Here, Christmas has a more intimate feel as simple strings of lights twinkle above narrow streets. You can observe people toting not only brightly wrapped packages but also baskets containing protruding baguettes, tins of *foie gras*, aged cheeses, and containers of oysters from their favorite neighborhood purveyors.

Christmas dinner is still largely eaten at home, with many families having a meal called the *reveillon* on Christmas Eve prior to midnight mass, and then having a larger dinner with the extended family on Christmas day. Appetizers generally consist of raw oysters, smoked salmon, or both. The main course is often a roast turkey or large capon served with a variety of vegetables and/or a green salad. Alternatively, goose and wild game may be served.

After dinner, there is always a cheese course, and finally dessert. The most traditional is the *bûche de Noël*, or Christmas log, which is a thin layer of sponge cake coated in chocolate, praline, or coffee-flavored cream frosting. The frosted cake is rolled, covered with more frosting, and then decorated to give the appearance of a log. Another dessert custom taken from the Provence region is the serving of thirteen desserts, mostly an assortment of nuts and dried fruits.

And not forgetting the true meaning of Christmas, the Hôtel de Ville proposes a beautiful *crèche*, or manger scene, every year in its massive courtyard, just next to a rink where ice-skating is possible. Others *crèches* are on display in churches throughout the city. Midnight mass at Notre-Dame is a classic event, and though it may be attended by invitation only, tourists can watch it on television from their hotel rooms.

For those who will spend Christmas in Paris for the first time this year, you will notice that from roughly December 23 to January 2, a blissful calm reigns everywhere. This is because Parisians leave town *en masse* to visit their family homes in the provinces. Diminished pedestrian and automobile traffic combines with early nightfall to allow for wonderful walks on which one can enjoy all the decorations and markets and the echo of church bells throughout the city without the hustle and bustle of crowds. Major avenues and tiny village-like *quartiers* await you. Huddled against the cold with a loved one on your arm, this is one of the most romantic experiences that the city can offer.

The Discover Paris!™ staff wishes you the happiest of holidays!

හ   ශ

The Eiffel Tower continues to sparkle for five minutes every evening on the hour.

Americans in Paris

La Closerie des Lilas

Hemingway's Paris
(2003)

Perhaps the most famous and frequently quoted American writer to live in Paris, Ernest Hemingway quipped that if one were lucky enough to have lived in Paris as a young man, then Paris would stay with him for the rest of his life.

Hemingway moved to Paris with his wife, Hadley, in 1921. He worked there as the European correspondent for the *Toronto Daily Star*, while making connections with writers and artists, and striving to become a published fiction writer. In his book *A Moveable Feast*, published posthumously in 1964, Hemingway recounts his experiences during those years in Paris, and writes about the people he met. While his prose is exuberant and nostalgic, it gives little insight into Paris and the French. Rather, the book is largely about how Hemingway reacted emotionally to the city. It relates amusing anecdotes about a number of the quite odd people (most of them American) whom he encountered and befriended.

The decade of the 1920s was a particularly intense and fertile period for writers and artists in Paris. Talented American writers such as Malcolm Cowley, Ezra Pound, and F. Scott Fitzgerald (to name only a few) gathered in and around the area called Montparnasse, frequenting cafés such as the Dôme and the Dingo where they exchanged ideas, argued, and drank. Hemingway was part of this scene, though he preferred the café called La Closerie des Lilas, where he could sit and write in relative tranquillity.

Through his association with writer Sherwood Anderson, Hemingway met other Americans living in Paris, a number of whom helped and encouraged him in his efforts to become a published writer. He met, for example, Gertrude Stein, who had been living in Paris since 1903. She reviewed Hemingway's manuscripts, and made comments on them, pronouncing some of them unprintable because of the frank language he used. Their friendship continued for some time, but soured by late 1926, perhaps due to rivalry. Hemingway gives his account of this falling-out in a chapter entitled "A Strange Enough Ending."

In another chapter, entitled "Hunger Was Good Discipline," Hemingway portrays himself as an impoverished writer during those early years. He relates how hunger was part of his experience while living in Paris, and how he used it to enhance his appreciation of the paintings of Cézanne that were on exhibit in the Luxembourg museum. According to Hemingway, Cézanne's works were sharper, clearer, and more beautiful when viewed on an empty stomach.

Later in this same chapter, he pays a visit to Sylvia Beach at her lending library, Shakespeare and Company, where he learns that a payment of 600 francs has arrived for one of his stories. Beach, seeing that he looks thin, encourages him to go home and have lunch. Instead, Hemingway immediately proceeds to the Brasserie Lipp, where he orders a potato salad and a liter of beer. The following paragraphs are a delicious account of a man enjoying a hearty meal, although one is left wondering whether Hadley was alone back at their apartment eating dry bread.

Travelers to Paris will enjoy reading this book before they embark on a trip to the city. Hemingway's stories will regale them and hone their anticipation of the delight that they will experience when walking in his footsteps and those of his friends.

Copying the Masters

(2006)

When we first met Jane, she told us that she was a copyist.
Having never heard of the profession before, we asked, "What does a copyist do?"

Jane said, "A copyist makes reproductions of the paintings of the masters. The idea is there, the composition is there, the colors are there. The only thing left for the copyist to do is to paint!"

We asked, "Why would anybody want a copy of a masterpiece?"

Jane said, "Because they can't afford the masterpiece."

All this sounded logical, and we were delighted when, a few weeks later, we received an invitation to the opening night of the *2e Salon des Copistes du Louvre*, which was being held at the town hall of the 6th *arrondissement* in Paris. We would see one of her works displayed there.

Although the exhibition room at the town hall was large, a bit of jostling was required to move through the enthusiastic crowd to view the paintings. The works of forty-five copyists were represented that night, including Jane's copy of *La Baigneuse*, by Jean-Auguste-Dominique Ingres (1808). Ingres is perhaps one of France's best-known painters of the nude female form; his eye-catching *Odalisque* (1814) brings tourists to a halt as they explore the Denon wing of the Louvre.

A scandal erupted on the night of the exhibition when a woman loudly protested the display of reproductions of the masters. Her opinion was that the reproductions amounted to forgery, and she was doubly scandalized to see counterfeits exhibited in the town hall. Jane carefully explained to her that the work of copyists is not forgery. For one thing, art enters the public domain if the artist has been dead for more than seventy-five years. For another, the work of a copyist must be at least 20 percent larger or smaller than the original work. Copyists who work in museums also receive an official museum stamp on the back of their canvases that certifies the work as a copy. Moreover, a forger would have to take great pains to make a copy that was indistinguishable from an original. He would have to paint on authentic old canvas, stretch the canvas on an authentic

Phase 1

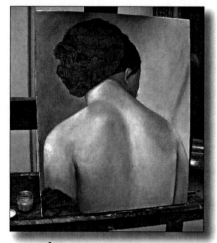

Phase 2

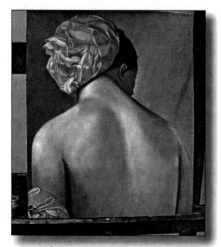

Phase 3

old frame, and use authentic paint from the era to fool the experts. A different profession altogether!

We asked Jane about the technique she used to achieve her superb copy of *La Baigneuse*. She gave us a few pointers.

Phase 1: A red ochre coat is used to hide the white canvas and give warmth to the undertone. This is called an "impression."

Phase 2: A "grisaille," or blocking in, of forms and shadows is done in grays, letting red show through.

Phase 3: The undercoat and grisaille are covered with colored glazes (transparent paint).

Phase 4: *Et voilà!*

Of course, it's not as easy as Jane makes it seem. She has been studying fine art, drawing, and painting in Paris for about ten years at the Ecole du Louvre, Ateliers de Beaux-Arts, Atelier de Saint-Paul, and the Académie de la Grande Chaumière, to name a few schools. She also studied restoration for two years.

Jane was first attracted to Paris during her years at the University of Washington (Seattle), when she decided to study French instead of math. A junior year abroad in Lausanne, Switzerland, gave her further exposure to French culture. After graduating from the university, she joined the Foreign Service of the State Department and was sent to Paris.

Returning to the States, she pursued a degree in education. She began teaching French, and subsequently became head of the foreign language department at a suburban school in Seattle. In 1980, still feeling the call of Paris, she decided to make the leap, and left for the City of Light. Her skills as a language teacher enabled her to find a position teaching English at the University of Paris. Later, she landed a corporate job as senior manager of communications with an international company. And she has never looked back!

Now, Jane works as a copyist at the Louvre, learning from the masters. She says, "Copying the masters, our teachers, is the way to learn to paint. There are approximately 160 copyists at the Louvre, but never all at the same time. The talents and levels of experience vary enormously, as witnessed by the recent *Salon des Copistes du Louvre.* It is a passion for all to be able to work within the walls of this hallowed institution. It is always a joy to talk with the tourists who seem, for the most part, fascinated by what we copyists are up to. The young children are especially candid, with questions like, 'Why are you painting another one?' I had a group of school kids watch me while I searched for that final stroke to make the smile on a portrait 'just so.' They gave me a standing ovation when I finally 'got it right!'"

Jane exhibits her copies at her studio. Among her works are copies of Rembrandt, Ingres, Vélasquez, Corot, Chardin, Gauguin, and Géricault. She also enjoys inserting the faces of her friends into replicas of portraits done by the masters, and creating personal greeting cards by painting her own face into one or more of those representations.

Louvre - Richelieu wing and pyramid

Sylvia Beach

(2004)

Among the many Americans who lived in Paris during the early part of the 20th century, the activities of one in particular had a profound influence on the literary movement that took shape there in the 1920s.

Sylvia Beach was fifteen years old when she first moved to Paris with her family in 1902. Her father, Sylvester Beach, had been assigned the duties of associate pastor of the American Church in Paris. She would later state that she and her sisters were extremely fond of Paris thanks to their parents, who took them there when they were very young. She lived in Paris for two years before returning to the United States in 1904.

The Beach sisters and their mother, Eleanor, would return to Europe again and again until finally Sylvia moved to Madrid with her mother in 1914. Apparently undeterred by the fact that France was at war, the two women traveled to Paris in August 1916 to join Beach's sister, Cyprian, who was establishing a successful film career there.

This marked Beach's final arrival in France, for she would not return to the United States with the exception of two visits, in 1936 and 1953, to see her family.

Another turning point in Beach's life occurred in 1917 when, while seeking a book of poetry by French poet Paul Fort, she came upon a bookshop on rue de l'Odéon run by a Frenchwoman named Adrienne Monnier. The two women, both sharing a strong admiration for French and American literature, became fast friends and collaborators on literary projects.

Two years later, with the help of Monnier and financing from Beach's mother, Beach opened her own bookshop (and lending library), called Shakespeare and Company, on nearby rue Dupuytren. The two shops complemented each other nicely, with Monnier's bookshop featuring modern French literature, and Beach's featuring modern English and American literature. Beach's shop quickly became a place where French, English, and American writers and readers would meet, forming close friendships and literary circles. Beach later moved her shop to 12, rue de l'Odéon, across the street from Monnier's bookstore.

It was through her literary connections that Beach met the Irish writer James Joyce in July 1920. Joyce had just moved to Paris from Trieste, Italy, at the urging of American writer Ezra Pound. And Beach, who admired the episodes of Joyce's *Ulysses* that had recently been published in Margaret Anderson's *The Little Review*, was reportedly awestruck to get the opportunity to meet him.

After their initial meeting, Joyce would pay visits to Beach at her bookshop. He would recount the troubles he was encountering in getting *Ulysses* published. His greatest problem seems to have been a legal complaint lodged by the New York Society for the Prevention of Vice against the publishers of *The Little Review*. A court enjoined them against publishing further installments. The ruling constituted a bar to publication of the completed work in either the United States or England.

In March 1921, while listening to Joyce recount the latest blow against getting his book published, Beach made the momentous decision to publish and distribute the book for him. Thus began a challenging and enduring effort to publish what has been called "a master work of modernist literature."

Apart from her efforts to publish Joyce's novel, Sylvia Beach played a central role in literary history in Paris throughout the 1920s and 1930s. She used her bookshop to promote young American writers, stocking and distributing their books and the magazines and reviews that contained their most recent works.

President Albert Lebrun of the French Republic admitted Beach into the Legion of Honor in 1938. A woman of tremendous energy and determination, she was finally forced to close her bookstore during the German occupation of the city in WWII. Refusing to leave town despite the Occupation, she was sent to an internment camp for six months. Immediately upon her release, she returned to Paris, where she remained until her death in 1962.

Travelers to Paris who wish to learn more about Sylvia Beach and the story of the American writers in Paris during the 1920s and 1930s may wish to consult *Sylvia Beach and the Lost Generation* by Noel Riley Fitch (New York: W. W. Norton & Company, 1985).

Photographing The Da Vinci Code
(2005)

Readers of Dan Brown's novel, *The Da Vinci Code*, whose curiosity leads them to search the Internet for information about the various locations mentioned in the mystery thriller, will likely come upon a Web site of stunning photography. The site is the creation of photographer David P. Henry, a Paris resident since 1996 and an ardent lover of the city. Henry had the good fortune to receive a commission from Doubleday to take photos for its latest edition of the bestseller *The Da Vinci Code: Special Illustrated Edition* (November 2004).

Though it was released in March 2003, Henry never heard of *The Da Vinci Code* before the spring of 2004, when he received an e-mail from a woman who was seeking photographs of Paris for Doubleday. She sent him a list of sites that she wanted photographed for the book, and he set about the task. It was only during the fulfillment of the assignment that he began to sense to what extent the book has become a worldwide phenomenon.

For example, while photographing Arago medallions embedded in the granite paving stones around the Comédie Française, he was approached, within the space of forty minutes, by more than a few tourists who asked if he knew about the book, or if he knew about guided *Da Vinci Code* walking tours. And in a humorous anecdote that Henry relayed during our interview, he described the experience of launching himself through the dense bushes that keep most people away from the surface of the Louvre's Inverted Pyramid, a skylight for the Carrousel du Louvre shopping mall underneath. While he was thrashing through the bushes, an American woman yelled over, "Are you looking for the Grail?"

Other sites for which Doubleday requested photographs were the Louvre pyramid (in the Cour Napoléon), the astronomical gnomon of Saint-Sulpice church, the Tuileries garden, and Sacré-Cœur Basilica. For his shots of the Louvre, Henry called the public affairs office of the museum to request permission to take pictures with a tripod. However, when he told the person at the office the reason for his request, she replied that she had read the book, that she understood perfectly why he wanted to take pictures, but that the answer to his request was categorically no. For

Pyramid viewed from Passage Richelieu

Inverted pyramid

the Louvre public affairs office, it seemed, *The Da Vinci Code* was already anathema!

It was not until after he finished the photo assignment that he read the novel and began to appreciate the impact of the ideas expressed in the book. "I enjoyed the book," he said. "It gives a lot of food for thought, especially in its account of the history of the Christian church. I think that it is good to have ideas challenged. I see a lot of synergy between *The Da Vinci Code* and the Monty Python film *The Life of Brian*."

Hailing from Boston, Henry first became interested in photography around the age of twelve. When he got to high school, he started using better cameras and studying darkroom technique. He took photographs for the creative arts magazine, the yearbook, and the school newsletter and calendar. He went on to study photography at the Massachusetts College of Art where he studied with Nicholas Nixon and Baldwin Lee, and received a Bachelor of Arts degree.

Henry's style of photography is unique, and his photos of Paris are unlike any you will find on the Internet. In describing his technique, he says, "I don't use a digital camera yet. As I have since forever, I still work with film, but for the last three years, I scan the negatives. Then, using Photoshop [professional editing software], I adjust color, brightness, and contrast, region by region. Photoshop also allows me to correct the distorted perspective seen in pictures of buildings."

With a solid background in photography, Henry found work within six months of arriving in France. "After two or three years, I didn't want to go back," he said. "Especially after G.W. got elected...."

Henry likes the city because it is big, yet maintains a human scale. He muses, "There are no skyscrapers, no canyons formed by buildings where the sunlight does not fall. Taking long walks in Paris gives you the feeling of walking from village to village. You have the wide-open sky and the sunlight above." He likes the shops that he sees as he walks, saying that they have appeal for the average pedestrian. They are not the offices of banks, tax consultants, or lawyers that one finds in New York, for example, but rather small shops, art galleries, cafés, grocery stores, and clothing stores.

He also likes the straightforward contact with culture and art that he experiences in Paris. "Artists and musicians pass through Paris on their way around Europe and the rest of the world. Just by staying in Paris you can see culture and art coming through the city month by month."

Though he did not state it specifically, one can also surmise that Henry likes Paris because of its diverse population. His favorite residential neighborhood is the Belleville district, where he lived for eight years. He describes it as "a neighborhood of immigration: there are plenty of people from other parts of Europe and Eastern Europe. There is also a significant Jewish population. The interesting thing here is that they are quite mixed in with the North Africans—there are plenty of restaurants in Belleville that offer both North African and Jewish cuisine... many Asians have moved to Belleville, to the point where the neighborhood has become known as another Chinatown."

Henry's appreciation of the beauty of the city is reflected in the photographs that he has published on his Web site, including a section of twenty-five photographs that appear in the illustrated edition of *The Da Vinci Code*. He also photographed Paris and its environs for the publication *Paris and Île de France Adventure Guide* (Hunter Publishing, 2004).

A few months ago, Henry began giving photography workshops in French and in English. Many participants have spent a weekend afternoon learning first about technical questions and camera settings, then spotting pictures and taking them out in the field.

Travelers to Paris will find inspiration in the many fine photographic images of the city that Henry has posted on his Web site. And fans of *The Da Vinci Code* will enjoy seeing photographs of places in Paris that are mentioned in the best-selling thriller.

୫୦   ୯୫

David P. Henry's Web address is www.davidphenry.com.

La Rotonde

Man and Juliet Ray
Photo from tombstone at
Montparnasse cemetery

Le Dôme

Homage to Man Ray
(2006)

Through photography, Man Ray (*né* Emmanuel Radnitsky) was perhaps the best known chronicler of the lives of artists, writers, and other creative spirits in early 20th-century Paris. Finding common cause with Parisian artists of the Dada movement who had come to New York, he left the US for Paris in 1921. Though he sought recognition as a painter there, it was his camera that would make him famous. The following walk celebrates his life by visiting his old haunts and recalling his remarkable career.

Man Ray's life in Paris began on the Right Bank in a café located in the passage de l'Opéra (now demolished) where Marcel Duchamp introduced him to the main players of Paris Dada. At that time, Ray had not envisioned making a life in France, but he soon decided to settle in Montparnasse, across the river. Even though he was a first-generation American born of Russian Jewish parents, with a less-than-perfect command of French, he felt at ease in this "cosmopolitan world" where "all languages were spoken, including French as terrible as my own."

Our walk begins at the Carrefour Vavin (now Place Pablo Picasso), which was the center of life in Montparnasse. When Man Ray first discovered the neighborhood, only two of the four cafés that now exist were present—Le Dôme and La Rotonde. While Le Dôme (108, boulevard du Montparnasse) was favored by Germanophones, Americans, and British, La Rotonde (105, boulevard du Montparnasse) was frequented by artists, writers, and political exiles from all nationalities and walks of life. It was the favorite hangout of Russian revolutionaries before the beginning of World War I—Leon Trotsky and Vladimir Lenin were regulars there. Among the artists were Picasso, Modigliani, and Foujita. Many of the artists were from Eastern Europe, and many of these were Jewish. They came to Paris seeking not only artistic inspiration, but also freedom from persecution.

Man Ray frequented both Le Dôme and La Rotonde. At La Rotonde, he met Kiki, his first Paris love.

Kiki (*née* Alice Prin [1901–1952]) worked as a model in this den of creativity. She had moved to Paris from Bourgogne in 1913. A frequent patron of the Rotonde, she met many of the artists for whom she posed at this café. She epitomized the new, independent woman of the 1920s, free from the traditional roles that society imposed. She often posed in the nude, and was painted and/or photographed by many who later became notable, including Chaim Soutine and Tsuguharu Foujita. She had a gregarious and generous nature, but could also display bad temper, particularly when aroused by jealousy. Man Ray would eventually immortalize her in numerous photos such as *Le Violon d'Ingres* and *Black and White*, as well as in the film *L'Etoile de Mer* (*Starfish*).

The street lying next to Le Dôme is rue Delambre. Up this street, at Number 15, is the Hôtel Lenox. Formerly known as the Hôtel des Ecoles, it became Man Ray's first Montparnasse home in December 1921. His room, Number 37, became a meeting place for the Dadaists as well as his workplace. That same month, he had the first one-man show of his paintings at the Surrealist bookstore Librairie Six in Paris' 7th *arrondissement*. Entitled "Exposition dada MAN RAY," it was a dismal failure. But during the show, Ray created one of his now famous Dada objects—an old-fashioned iron with tacks glued to the flat surface that he called *The Gift* (replica held at the Museum of Modern Art, New York).

Dada was a literary and artistic movement based on the principles of deliberate irrationality, anarchy, cynicism, and the rejection of laws of beauty and social organization. Man Ray described it as negative and destructive. When Surrealism began to supplant Dadaism in 1922, he was there to play a role in defining this new movement. He would make a name for himself that year as a portraitist and the inventor of "Rayographs," working out of the makeshift darkroom in his hotel room.

From Number 15, rue Delambre, proceed up the street, and turn left to enter boulevard Edgar Quinet. Crossing the boulevard, turn left and walk down the street to the main entrance to the Montparnasse cemetery at Number 3. This is Man Ray's final resting place.

The grave is located in Plot Number 7, along the avenue de l'Ouest. This area is a jumble of headstones, but Man Ray's tomb can be identified by the photos of him and his wife, Juliet, that sit atop it. Juliet was married to Ray from 1946 until his death; she was buried with him in 1991. Tristan Tzara, father of Dada and hotel mate of Man Ray, is buried in neighboring Plot Number 8, and Surrealist poet Robert Desnos is buried in the long, thin Plot Number 15 on the right side of avenue de l'Ouest.

Leaving the cemetery by the main entrance, turn right and walk to the corner of boulevard Edgar Quinet and boulevard Raspail. Turn right, walk the short distance to the first crosswalk, and cross boulevard Raspail to enter rue Campagne Première. On the right, near the corner, the building at Numbers 31 and 31bis is covered with glazed tiles. Man Ray moved to Number 31bis during the summer of 1922. His ground-floor studio was small, but included a loggia that he used as a bedroom and darkroom. Here, he continued to ply his trade as a portraitist, photographing people such as

Henri Matisse, Nancy Cunard, and Gertrude Stein in his studio. By this time, he was earning enough money from photography to begin giving away his paintings.

At Number 29, the Hôtel Istria still operates. Man Ray rented a room at the hotel so that he would have more privacy for himself and for Kiki while freeing the studio at 31bis to be entirely devoted to work. His friend Marcel Duchamp eventually moved there as well.

Farther down the street on the left, at the corner of boulevard du Montparnasse, was the American-owned bar The Jockey (Number 146, boulevard du Montparnasse). Man Ray photographed the inauguration, even managing to get into the group photo himself by setting the shutter to activate after a brief delay. Kiki began to sing there, and quickly became the toast of the quarter.

Turn left onto boulevard du Montparnasse and proceed down the street. Number 132 was the address of the magazine *Paris Montparnasse*, run by journalist Henri Broca. Broca published a caricature of Kiki and Man Ray, depicting Ray as a pint-sized figure trailing a well-endowed Kiki. His caption likened Man Ray to a lap dog. Kiki would leave Man Ray for Broca during their collaboration on the publication of her memoirs in 1929.

Returning to Place Pablo Picasso, you arrive once again at Le Dôme. A friend and photographic subject, Jacqueline Barsotti, once found Man Ray here feeling very depressed over the breakup of his relationship with Lee Miller. Barsotti may have dissuaded him from committing suicide that night. Man Ray would eventually turn his anguish over the separation into a painting entitled *A l'heure de l'observatoire, les Amoureux* (1932–1934), which depicts Miller's lips floating above a Paris landscape.

Our walk ends farther along the boulevard at the youngest of the Carrefour Vavin cafés—La Coupole (Number 102, boulevard du Montparnasse). Man Ray shifted his allegiance from Le Dôme to La Coupole in 1928, in the company of Jacqueline Barsotti. His preferred table was Number 56.

Since Man Ray's death in 1976, there have been at least 174 one-man exhibitions of his works in art galleries and museums around the world.

The Centre Pompidou in Paris received Man Ray's entire photographic archive in 1994. It holds many other Dada works as well. The section of the museum that displays the majority of these works is currently closed for renovation; it is scheduled to reopen during the first quarter of 2007.

જ્ઞ   ૠ

The sections of the Pompidou that display Man Ray's works
(Levels 4 and 5) have been reopened to the public.

Juan Sánchez

La Dernière Goutte

Wine stock

Wining and Dining with Juan Sánchez

(Excerpts)

(2006)

Juan Sánchez is an American expat with a passion for food and wine. He moved to Paris from Miami, volunteered in restaurant kitchens for a couple of years, returned to Miami, and then settled permanently in Paris. He attended a prestigious culinary school upon his return, but instead of going back into the restaurant arena after graduation, he opened a wine store. Since 1996 he has been operating La Dernière Goutte, his second wine shop in the Saint-Germain-des-Prés quarter. Three years later he returned to cooking when he opened a restaurant, Fish, just a block away. Discover Paris!™ recently had the opportunity to talk with him about his experiences in the City of Light.

DP: What inspired you to come to Paris?

JS: Working in my dad's company, I decided "You're young… time to go." My father had a food-service distribution business, supplying restaurants, hotels, Club Meds with food products. I don't like distribution—I like retail and I like people… I like people coming to me as opposed to having to cold-call clients.

DP: So then, you were working in your father's business. Did your father think you would take it over?

JS: Well, that was basically what I was doing. I was actually running the company with my dad. My dad has always been supportive with me and with all my siblings, saying that we should do whatever we want.

DP: So then you thought *Well, I'll go to Paris?*

JS: Yeah, pretty much. During my freshman year at university, my brothers and my first cousin and I all did three months of travel to Europe. That was quite an experience for an eighteen-year-old. I only stayed one day in Paris—it was at the tail end of our trip. When I took my real-estate courses at the university, I also took a course in French. I had taken two semesters of French in high school prior to that. So French is always something that I've been interested in.

I moved to Paris in 1989. I had saved money and planned to stay indefinitely. I would eat in restaurants, and if I liked the food, I would ask if I could work there for free and show up the next morning. I would work there for as little as a day or as much as two or three weeks. It was more observation of what went on in the kitchen as opposed to a real position. I did some bookkeeping at a huge *charcuterie* and got to learn how to make *pâtés*. The worst thing is seeing how *andouillette* is made and having to clean out the intestines! You quickly go vegetarian!

But after about one and half to two years—money doesn't last as long one thinks—I went back to Miami, worked for my dad for a year, then I returned to France, having signed up for a chef school—the Ecole Grégoire Ferrandi. It is probably *the* school in Paris for anybody getting into professional cooking.

DP: How did you become interested in wine?

JS: Food has really been my interest. Right after chef school, I met a woman who ran a *charcuterie* in the Buci market. She had a space next to her business from which she sold wines, but not quality wines. We formed a company together, and I took over the wine shop, which was called Les Bioux. I learned about wine little by little by going to lots of professional tastings in Paris, talking with and tasting wines with winemakers. It was the winemakers who really helped me along.

When my silent partner wanted a more active role in the business, I left to start my own business. I opened La Dernière Goutte in October of 1996, three months after leaving Les Bioux. (La Dernière Goutte is located in a 300-year-old building—the storefront is a classified historical site.)

DP: Do you visit the vineyards of the winemakers whose wines you sell?

JS: I travel quite a bit for regional tastings. The Vinexpo at Bordeaux and the Vinisud at Montpellier are important events that are held every other year. We go to the satellite expos at these events because they are smaller and more concentrated. And because the French wine industry is suffering from too much supply, winemakers make a huge effort to have tastings in Paris. Between January and April there are at least two or three professional tastings every Monday in Paris. There is no reason why any restaurant in Paris should not have a personalized wine list.

DP: What percentage of the wines that you sell are artisanal [locally produced wines using traditional methods]?

JS: I stock 400 wines. Only five or six are foreign [non-French] ones. Ninety percent of the wines I sell are artisanal. I like this market because I can deal direct with smaller vineyards and independent winemakers. A number of these producers are women.

DP: Is the French concept of *terroir* [the notion that wine is an expression of its soil and climate] something that you endorse? This is a concept that many Americans don't seem to understand or embrace.

JS: Yes! It is what *makes* French wines and is the number-one difference between French and American wines. No doubt about it. If American winemakers want to progress in the quality of their wines, they will need to get more of the influence of the soil into their products. Of course, they already have soil. But they need to get the expression of that soil into the wine. I am not talking about quality, because quality is subjective. American wines are well made and they have a specific style. But I prefer French wines because they have a lot more depth and complexity, and this comes from the soil.

DP: Do the winemakers who come to your shop every Saturday for your weekly tastings come to see you or do they come to interact with your clients?

JS: I invite them to come up. They are not allowed to present all their wines, but rather the ones that I select from their inventory. I almost require that the winemakers whom I deal with come up to the shop—I visit them and purchase their wines throughout the year, so I think that the least that they can do is come up and spend a Saturday at La Dernière Goutte. We start in the morning, then break for a good lunch at Fish, then return to the wine shop in the afternoon. It's partially social and partly commercial.

DP: Would you start a wine shop in the States?

JS: No. It's not the same business. In France you have the possibility to interact directly with the winemaker if you desire.

DP: When did you open Fish?

JS: In January 1999. I started out as the chef; now another chef prepares the food. We made a decision for reasons of the health of our staff to make the restaurant nonsmoking in January 2006. The restaurant seats fifty-five to fifty-eight persons. We are planning to introduce organic foods and herbal teas in our menu.

We are thinking of expanding this year.

DP: At Fish, how much of your clientele is American?

JS: It can be all French one night, all American the next. Definitely the first seating is American. At 9:30, 10:00 p.m., the French begin piling in. And I think that is really the sign of our success today, because even when tourism is down, we're still full. We've been very lucky to have good reviews in *Le Figaro* and many guidebooks, which really helps. We are also lucky to be in this area, which is really one of the heartbeats of Paris. And we produce very good food, which is a great advantage in this area of touristy restaurants.

DP: What made you decide to change Fish to a 100 percent nonsmoking restaurant?

JS: We had been thinking about it for a while, and we hesitated because we thought people would think that the restaurant was "too American." But for us, we got home every night with clothes that smelled like smoke. We were smoking… we were smoking I don't know how many cigarettes a night. It was a health decision. And the future of Fish is going to be tied to such decisions—getting into sustainable fishing, going as organic as possible, getting into herbal teas and incorporating medicinal herbs into our dishes.

And it's turned out that smokers are not really a good clientele—they sit over a cup of espresso for forty minutes and smoke a cigarette while twenty people are lined up waiting for a table. The new policy is great for turning over tables. Not to mention that we have eliminated the possibility of accidentally starting fires in the waste bins due to cigarette butts that have not been completely extinguished. There have been a few times when we've asked ourselves what was burning, and it turned out to be the trash!

Now, our smoking clientele get up and go out to the front of the restaurant when they want to smoke. There is something quite lively about this—they get up, they smoke, you see little relationships forming outside the window, especially with the pretty women who go outside. Occasionally, even a nonsmoker will go out to strike up conversation with a woman: "So, smoke here often?"

DP: Your façade is conducive to that kind of activity.

JS: Well, the façade is classified. It is one hundred years old. It used to be a *poissonerie* and we changed the "p" to a "b" for *boissonerie*. The word "*boissonerie*" does not exist in French, but we've been in so many newspapers because of this, and every day, there are a minimum of two to three people who come to the restaurant just to take a picture of the façade.

La Dernière Goutte
6, rue de Bourbon le Château
75006 Paris
Tel: 01.43.29.11.62
Metro: Mabillon or Odéon

Fish, la Boissonerie (Mediterranean cuisine)
69, rue de Seine
75006 Paris
Tel: 01.43.54.34.69
Metro : Mabillon or Odéon

ജ   ഃ

As of 1 January 2008, all eating establishments in France are nonsmoking.

Churches and Cathedrals

Notre-Dame Cathedral

East Meets West
at Notre-Dame Cathedral
(2005)

Easter was celebrated in March this year, with the Lenten season beginning on February 9. Notre-Dame Cathedral, the *grande dame* of Paris churches, scheduled many events in preparation for this, the holiest day of the Christian calendar. Among them, and perhaps the most special, were weekly ceremonies of the Veneration of the Crown of Thorns.

Paris is home to three important physical representations of Christ's Passion: the Crown of Thorns, a piece of the Cross of Christ, and a Nail of the Passion. These are kept in the sacristy at Notre-Dame. The Crown, perhaps the most treasured relic in all of Christendom, is usually presented for veneration on the first Friday of each month. During Lent, however, ceremonies are held every Friday.

In 1239, King Louis IX purchased the Crown and other relics from the Latin emperor of Byzantium, Baudouin II. When the Crown arrived in Paris, the king organized a grand procession to carry it to Notre-Dame Cathedral for a ceremony. Soon afterward, he built a royal chapel, Sainte-Chapelle, to protect and display the relics.

Hundreds of years later, during the French Revolution, the relics that the king had collected at Sainte-Chapelle were confiscated. The Crown of Thorns was taken to the National Library, and then transferred to Notre-Dame Cathedral in 1805. It has remained there since that date.

The Crown of Thorns is a band of woven rushes sealed in a circular tube, twenty-one centimeters in diameter. Tradition holds that the thorns were manually incorporated into the meshwork formed by the rushes. None remain today; Byzantium emperors and French kings dispersed them as gifts over the centuries.

On March 4, the fourth Friday of Lent this year, an Orthodox vespers service was held at Notre-Dame during the Veneration of the Crown. Hieromonk Nestor, rector of the Russian parish under the patriarchate of Moscow, presided over the ceremony. A group of choristers directed by Protodeacon Alexandre Kedroff, cantor and choirmaster of Saint-Alexandre-Nevski Cathedral in Paris, provided vocal accompaniment. The choir comprised members of the Kedroff Vocal Ensemble

Saint-Alexandre-Nevski Cathedral

and other singers recruited for the occasion. During the ceremony, their voices filled Notre-Dame with stirring hymns from the liturgical tradition of the Eastern Orthodox Church. Kedroff and his ensemble were invited to participate in the veneration ceremony at Notre-Dame through the initiative of the clergy of the patriarchate of Moscow.

Prior to the commencement of the ceremony, the choristers assembled behind the altar. The roughly ninety-minute observance began with organ music announcing the beginning of a large procession of clergy and others, including four women dressed in black from head to foot, their faces covered by veils. The priest who led the procession swung a censer, perfuming the air with incense. Hieromonk Nestor walked in the middle of the procession, dressed in regal purple robes with gold trim, his head coiffed with a black cap called a *klobouk*. Each of the three relics of the Passion (the Crown, the piece of the Cross, and the Nail) was carried by a different member of the clergy. The procession began in the transept on the north aisle, circled around to the front of the church, and made its way up the center aisle to the altar. There the relics were displayed, and the participants took their places for the service.

For this special ceremony, Hieromonk Nestor and the choristers sang liturgical chants from "The Exaltation of the Holy Cross," one of the twelve "great feasts" of the Orthodox Church traditionally performed each year on September 14. Unaccompanied by musical instruments, the clear, rich voices of the all-male choir reverberated through the nave and transept and under the arches of Paris' most famous cathedral. The chants were sung in Slavonic, with a brief translation given in French. After the presentation, the congregation was invited, row by row, to file up to the altar to view and kiss the Crown.

Hieromonk Nestor

Protodeacon Kedroff, the leader of the choristers, is the grandson of Nicolas Kedroff, founder of the Kedroff Quartet. The quartet, founded in 1897 in Saint Petersburg, gave a number of concerts throughout Europe from 1908 to 1915. With the advent of the Russian Revolution, Kedroff's grandfather immigrated to Paris, where he reconstituted his ensemble. The son of the founder, also named Nicolas, continued the tradition of ancient chants of the Russian church. By 1975 the group had performed 3,000 concerts in Europe and the United States.

After the death of the second-generation Nicolas, Alexandre Kedroff founded a new ensemble (now with seven singers), devoted to Russian liturgical chants and a number of old popular Russian songs of religious inspiration. In 2001 the Kedroff Vocal Ensemble won the Grand Prize of the 6th International Festival of Orthodox Music held in Minsk.

The Kedroff Vocal Ensemble continues the tradition of its founder by giving performances throughout France and Europe. It has produced three CD recordings of liturgical chant; however distribution of the albums is limited to their sale in the vestibule of the magnificent Saint-Alexandre-Nevski Cathedral, located at 12, rue Daru in Paris. A sample of liturgical music from "The Exaltation of the Holy Cross" (performed by a different choir) can be found at the Web site:

http://www.goarch.org/en/special/listen_learn_share/exaltholycross/listen/.

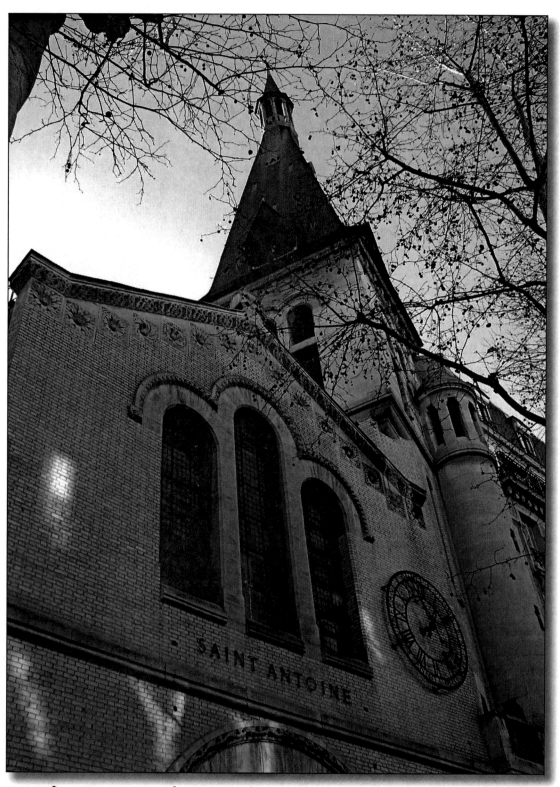

Eglise Saint-Antoine des Quinze-Vingts

Christian Churches in Paris

(2003)

by Monique Y. Wells

In July, we bid farewell to the season of Christian holidays such as Easter Monday, Ascension Day, and Pentecost Monday that prolong weekends and ease us into summer. I was thinking about these religious celebrations when I came upon the first of a number of unusual places of worship during my meanderings around the city.

Several days ago, I decided to take a different route home from the rue des Ecoles, and turned up the rue des Carmes for a brief but challenging walk up Sainte-Geneviève hill toward the Pantheon. To my left, I saw a small building that resembled a chapel. When I approached the gate, I saw from the affixed plaque that it is a church called Saint-Ephrem, and that the congregation is Syrian. The sign bears a foreign script (Syrian or Arabic) as well as Roman lettering. Fascinated, I entered, and encountered two priests who were conversing in heavily accented French. The interior is decorated very simply, but boasts a beautifully ornate rood screen carved in wood. This is one of the few such screens remaining in Paris, most of them having been destroyed during the French Revolution.

To learn more about this church, I took a flyer from the table adjacent to the entrance. It is named after Saint Ephrem the Syrian, who lived from AD 306 to 373. Its parish consists of over 350 families of Syrian, Iraqi, Turkish, and Egyptian origin. Mass is celebrated in Syrian, Arabic, and French. The prayer book is written in phonetic Arabic and Syrian, and is accompanied by a translation for non-Syrians who attend services here.

The next day, while heading toward the Café Marly for a lovely lunch on the terrace, I happened upon a building on the rue de Lille that bears the words *"Eglise Baptiste."* Because the word *"église"* generally indicates a Catholic church, I was intrigued by the inscription and walked over to the building to investigate. Upon entering the hall that leads to a tiny courtyard, I found a poster indicating that the principal worshipers here are Protestant, and are members of an evangelical movement called La Fédération des Eglises Evangéliques Baptistes (the Federation of Evangelical Baptist Churches). My curiosity was further aroused when I saw a sign

Église Saint-Ephrem

with the words *"Berger d'Israël"* and another written in Chinese! When I inquired about this, I learned that the Berger d'Israël is an association that offers Christian testimony to Jews, and that a Chinese community worships at this address.

The string of discoveries did not stop there. The following day, I went to the *quartier* Saint-Germain-des-Prés to photograph a few sites of interest on the rue des Saints-Pères. I came across an old church on the corner of this street and boulevard Saint-Germain, whose façade is almost black from lack of restoration. As I approached, the congregation was exiting the church, and I heard the lilting voices of a girls' chorus. Having always been curious about this place, I went inside. I learned that it is a Ukrainian Orthodox church called Saint-Vladimir-le-Grand.

Plaques in Ukrainian and in French displayed on either side of the double doors inside the vestibule tell of this church's interesting history. It was formerly the chapel of a hospital called La Charité. Simon Petlura, former president of the Democratic Republic of the Ukraine and Supreme Commander of its armies, was mortally wounded on rue Racine by an assassin who opposed the independent Ukraine. Transported to the hospital at this site, Petlura died here on May 25, 1926. Years later, the hospital was destroyed and the chapel made into a church that was dedicated to the Ukrainian community.

A day later, while making my way to the café L'Arrosoir on avenue Daumesnil for another lunch date, I noticed a tower topped with a cross looming above the Viaduc des Arts on avenue Ledru Rollin. The tower faces the street at an unusual angle, and as I approached, I could see a wrought-iron clock on the façade of the building. This neo-Roman church, which dates from 1903, is dedicated to Saint-Antoine des Quinze-Vingts (Saint Anthony of the Fifteen-Twenties—a reference to the 300-bed hospice that Louis IX created to care for the blind in 1260). It boasts an organ made by Aristide Cavaillé-Coll, who also created the famous organs at Saint-Sulpice, La Madeleine, and Notre-Dame de Paris.

Last October, forty-seven members of this parish made a pilgrimage to Lebanon to forge a relationship with the Menorite parish of Saint-Antoine-le-Grand in Beirut. Next to the entrance of the church in Paris, a plaque commemorates the official commencement of this relationship, which took place on January 17, 2004.

Every church in Paris has a unique story, and foreign communities are an integral part of many of them. The Web site Catholic Paris (www.catholique-paris.com; in French) lists over twenty nationalities that practice Catholicism in Paris, including Portuguese, Haitian, Japanese, Latin American, and Mauritian. Two Protestant evangelical organizations operate in Paris—the one mentioned above and a second one called L'Association Evangélique d'Eglises Baptistes de Langue Française (The Evangelical Association of French-Language Baptist Churches). Membership in evangelical churches is growing due to increased participation by African and Caribbean immigrants. Lutherans, Episcopalians, and other Protestants also worship in the city. As is true for so many other cultural aspects of life, Christian churches reflect the rich and diverse nature of the Paris population.

Cupola fresco by Pierre Mignard

The Church of Val-de-Grâce
(2007)

There exists in Paris a remarkable church whose interior is so beautiful and sumptuous that first-time visitors cannot fail to feel a sense of exultation upon entering its sanctuary. Yet the church, Val-de-Grâce, is not frequented by large numbers of tourists. Many are probably unaware of its location, for it lies in a vicinity that was chosen for its relative isolation—the faubourg Saint-Jacques.

In the 17th century, this area lay in a district outside of the walls of Paris that had been settled by a number of religious orders, including the Ursulines, Feuillantines, and Capucins. As was sometimes the case in those times, a queen or noblewoman would take a convent under her protection, and sponsor the construction or renovation of its buildings. In this tradition, Queen Anne of Austria, consort of Louis XIII, provided financial support to a Benedictine convent that was eventually named the Royal Abbey of Val-de-Grâce.

The years between which Anne was established as founder of the convent (by letters of patent of the king in 1621) and was finally able to provide financial support (after 1643, following the death of the king and her appointment as regent of France) were frustrating. Her marriage to Louis XIII in 1615 had been arranged between the Bourbons of France and the Habsburgs of Spain, and by 1637 she had not borne Louis a child. Producing no male offspring would have had serious consequences for the continuity of the Bourbon dynasty and serious personal consequences for her. To add to her vexations, Richelieu, the king's prime minister, spied on her, suspecting that she was secretly communicating with her brother, Philip IV of Spain.

In fact, she was.

Anne made frequent trips to the convent and would stay several days there. In this presumably safe environment, she passed letters to intermediaries, one of whom was eventually arrested. Subsequent to an investigation, the queen was forced to sign a humiliating confession, and was banned from entering convents without the express permission of the king.

The birth of her son, Louis XIV, in 1638 was a source of great joy for her. So

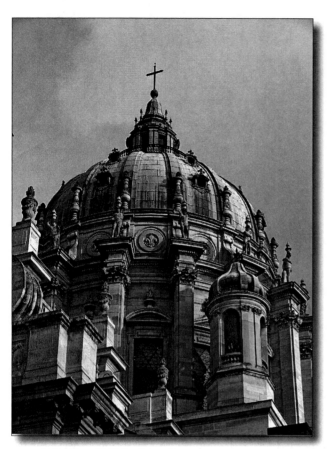

Cupola of Val-de-Grâce

greatly had she desired a son, in fact, that she vowed to reconstruct the convent and to build a magnificent church, dedicating it to the Nativity, if God would grant her this gift. On April 8, 1645, seven-year-old Louis XIV posed the first stone for the church. Ten years later his younger brother, the Duke of Anjou, born in 1640, posed the first stone for the new convent.

Val-de-Grâce is a marvel to behold, displaying a number of intriguing architectural elements that deserve our attention. The structure is attributed to the work of at least four prominent architects of the era: initially François Mansart, and subsequently, Jacques Lemercier, Gabriel Le Duc, and Pierre Le Muet.

The church stands in a large cobblestone courtyard behind magnificent iron gates. The initial building project included the construction of a great semicircular forecourt in front of the iron gates, designed to display the church to its best effect. But this forecourt was never built, and the street that was pierced along the east-west axis in front of the church (rue du Val-de-Grâce, built from 1797 to 1811) is not wide enough to permit a grand perspective.

The façade of the church consists of two levels. The lower level sits above a stairway whose sixteen steps rise up to the porch. Over the porch, supported by four Corinthian columns, stands a pediment that rests on an architrave bearing the Latin inscription JESU NASCENTI VIRGINIQUE MATRI (To the Newborn Jesus and the Virgin Mother). The tympanum displays the monogram AL, which signifies Anne and Louis XIII. The second level of the façade bears some similarity to the first, except that the middle portion of the base of its wide pediment is recessed, and its supporting columns display the Composite order. The tympanum of the second level displays the coat of arms of Anne of Austria. Inverted consoles flank the second level, giving the façade a decidedly 16th-century Italian appearance.

Behind the façade towers a cupola. The latter rests on a great drum, which in turn rests on a cubic base. The drum is flanked by four turrets and pierced by sixteen tall windows, each of which is crowned by a rounded or triangular pediment. Between the windows stand buttresses surmounted by statues of human figures balancing firepots on their heads. On top of the cupola rises a lantern encircled by an iron balustrade and topped by a sphere of bronze and, finally, a cross. When first built, the cupola was embellished with gold paint. When it was renovated, the gilt was not replaced.

Upon entering the church one is struck by its sober beauty. The ceiling of the nave is entirely of carved, vaulted stone, displaying images of

Nave

63

Saint Joachim and Saint Anne (the parents of the Virgin Mary), the Virgin Mary and Saint Joseph (the parents of Christ), and Saint Zachary and Saint Elizabeth (the parents of John, the cousin of Christ). Each saintly image is flanked by tiny angels, with those flanking the male saints standing and those flanking the female saints sitting. A careful observer will note that the frames of the carvings on the ceiling are reflected in the marquetry on the marble floor. This repetition of design is extraordinary to behold, and the visitor's eyes will shift continually up to the ceiling and down to the floor to seek confirmation that the opposing patterns are indeed precise images of one another.

Between the nave and the chancel stands a wrought-iron gate whose presence recalls the medieval custom of separating the clergy from the worshipers by means of a rood screen. The gate was designed by architects Le Muet and Le Duc, and was once adorned with *fleurs de lys* and royal monograms. These symbols of royal authority were removed during the French Revolution.

Beneath the dome at the eastern end of the nave rises a great baldaquin, under which stands the high altar. The baldaquin consists of six wreathed columns of black marble embellished with gilded bronze leaves and palm fronds. Posed on the high altar is a Nativity scene depicting Mary on the left, the Christ Child in the middle, and Joseph on the right. This group was originally sculpted by Michel Anguier, and is considered to be his masterpiece. It was moved out of the church into hiding to preserve it from destruction during the French Revolution. The sculpted group that stands here is a 19th-century copy; the original now stands in the Saint-Roch church on rue Saint-Honoré.

Miraculously preserved, too, was the marble floor of the cupola, with its swirling pattern of lozenges and the central monogram of Anne of Austria. Before Revolutionary forces arrived to strip the church of its furnishings and destroy symbols of the crown, church caretakers took the precaution to cover the floor with

Marble floor

64

a layer of plaster and strew it with straw. Thanks to their foresight, the floor was spared, and today we can marvel at its beauty.

If we needed to speak in superlatives, the *pièce de résistance* would unquestionably be the fresco of the cupola that unfurls above the baldaquin. Painted by Pierre Mignard, the scene depicts an ascending spiral of the blessed rising upon clouds into an increasingly dazzling paradise, in whose center lies the Holy Trinity. Among the whorl of church fathers, prophets, virgins, and martyrs, we see the kneeling Anne of Austria, with crown at her feet, offering her church heavenward in a supplicating gesture. Surely this image speaks more about devotion to her faith than any words could ever convey.

The church is open to the public for Sunday mass. On Tuesdays, Wednesdays, Saturdays, and Sundays access is possible between noon and 6:00 p.m. through the Musée du Service de Santé des Armées. Entry into the museum is 5€.

Organ at Saint-Sulpice

Saint-Sulpice

(2006)

M any a visitor to Saint-Sulpice church must think its façade remarkably odd. Its ground-floor portico is flanked by two towers that have no particular elegance, and the portico itself is topped by a massive loggia that greatly resembles the portico beneath it. This redundancy gives the façade a wide, squat appearance, contrary to the edifying, uplifting vision of earlier Gothic churches. Moreover, the south tower looks unfinished, and indeed it is—the French Revolution put an end to the architect's plans to complete it. A pediment located between the towers once gave the façade the appearance of altitude, but lightning destroyed the pediment in 1770. Thus the overall appearance of the façade is one of heaviness rather than loftiness.

Another attribute that is vexing to the eye is the steps that lead up to the portico. Normally, steps are designed to lead *up* to the columns that stand on the portico. In contrast, the steps at Saint-Sulpice rise *between* the columns, depriving the façade of a grand stairway, and giving it a foreshortened appearance.

Foreshortened and squat! Upon viewing a façade like this, should one even consider entering to see the interior?

By all means, yes! For the façade belies the elegance and grace that are found within.

The construction of Saint-Sulpice church dates from the 17th and 18th centuries, a period when Gothic architecture had been abandoned and was even despised. The interior of the church (as well as its façade) reflects a desire to return to classical forms. Upon entering the nave the visitor will find inspiration in soaring, fluted Corinthian pilasters and a catenary (high-arched) ceiling.

The desire to reject Gothic architecture also extended to the rejection of the dark stained-glass windows of that period. The windows of Saint-Sulpice do not "tell a story" as Gothic windows did, and the rich colors of that era have been discarded. The stained-glass windows in this church were designed to let an abundance of natural light enter through the arched windows above the cornice.

A number of renowned artists were commissioned to embellish the interior of

Saint-Sulpice. Upon entering, the visitor will note three works by Eugène Delacroix (painted from 1850 to 1861) in the Chapel of the Holy Angels immediately to the right. These paintings depict rather violent scenes. On the ceiling, the Archangel Saint Michel is poised to thrust a spear between the ribs of a demon. To the right, Heliodore receives a sound thrashing, and, on the left, Jacob wrestles with an angel. Delacroix is perhaps best known for his work *Liberty Guiding the People*, on display at the Louvre.

To the left of the entrance stands one of two holy water fonts fashioned from the shell of a giant clam—the *Tridacna gigas*—mounted on a marble pedestal sculpted in *rocaille* style by Jean-Baptiste Pigalle, one of the most popular sculptors of the 18th century. The clamshells were given to King François I in the 16th century by the Venetian Republic. Pigalle also sculpted the large statue of Mary located in the Chapel of the Blessed Virgin at the far end of the church.

The altar lies under a magnificent cupola supported by four ornate pendentives decorated with sculpted, low-relief firepots. The cupola itself displays four medallions with images of Christ (to the east), Melchisedech (to the west), Saint Peter (to the north) and Saint John the Baptist (to the south), as well as a dove of peace (carrying an olive branch) that radiates glory.

Among the notable furnishings of the high altar are six gilded bronze candlesticks by Louis-Isidore Choiselat, who was a renowned specialist of cast bronze altarpieces in the 19th century. As well as supplying the candlesticks for Saint-Sulpice in 1825, Choiselat obtained the prestigious order for altarpieces for the coronation of Charles X in Reims earlier in the same year. The candlesticks for Saint-Sulpice were modeled after the ones for the coronation. Standing five feet tall, each candlestick is tripodal with claw feet. The base has three angel heads at the topmost angles, and supports a column adorned with vine leaves and plant stalks. The candle holder at the top of the column is decorated with ornamental leaves.

Readers of the popular novel *The Da Vinci Code* will recognize these candlesticks, one of which is referred to in the novel as a "heavy iron votive candle holder." In the novel, the fanatical monk Silas seizes the candle holder and uses it to batter a hole through the surface of the floor at a spot near the marble obelisk that stands against the wall of the north transept. This obelisk is an element of an astronomical project initiated by the parish priest Languet de Gergy in 1727. Languet wanted an instrument to determine the exact moment of equinoxes and solstices so that Easter day could be calculated. (According to astronomical rules, Easter falls on the first Sunday after the full moon that occurs after the vernal equinox.)

Languet ordered the construction of a gnomon, which is normally a shaft perpendicular to the horizon, but in this case is a small hole pierced in the window of the south transept. Whereas the shaft would cast a shadow as the sun moves across the sky, the hole in the window permits a beam of light to pass through, casting a circular image on the floor or wall of the church. As the image sweeps from west to east across the transept, it crosses a brass meridian line running from a marble plaque in the south transept to the top of the obelisk in the north transept. In the summer, when the sun is at its highest, the image falls on the marble plaque. In the winter, when the sun is at its lowest, the image crosses the meridian line at a point marked by the zodiacal sign of Capricorn engraved in the upper portion of the obelisk. And during the spring and fall equinoxes, the image falls on the meridian line at the location of an oval copper plaque that lies behind the balustrade of the altar.

Looking back to the entrance of the church from the transept, one can view a splendid organ case. This was designed in 1776 by architect Jean-François Chalgrin, who is perhaps best known for his design of the Arc de Triomphe (located at the top of avenue des Champs-Elysées). The organ itself was built by François-Henri Clicquot (completed in 1781 with sixty-four stops), but restored by Aristide Cavaillé-Coll in 1846 (with one hundred stops). After its restoration, the organ of Saint-Sulpice was hailed as one of the three great "hundred-stop" organs of Europe, a "masterwork of modern organ building."

Daniel Roth has been titular organist of this magnificent instrument since 1985. During a recent mass held on Palm Sunday, he played improvisations on *Hosanna filio David* and *Ardemment j'aspire à une fin heureuse* (by Johannes Brahms) as well as *O Homme pleure sur tes lourds péchés* (by Jean-Sébastian Bach).

A sample of Roth's music can be heard at www.stsulpice.com/Docs/video/improv1.rm. The music program of Saint-Sulpice is found at www.stsulpice.com/Docs/concerts.html.

Saint-Sulpice church—a feast for the eyes, a glorious concert for the ears, and inspiration for the soul!

Eglise Saint-Germain-l'Auxerrois

The King's Church
(2007)

Travelers to Paris strolling along the broad rue de l'Amiral de Coligny might not initially spot the Eglise Saint-Germain-l'Auxerrois, hidden behind a row of trees on the place du Louvre. Their attention would be drawn first to the grand Colonnade du Louvre that was built in the 17th century to serve as the main entrance to the Louvre Palace. Their eyes might then turn to the Mairie of the 1st *arrondissement*, a 19th-century municipal administrative building designed to look like a church; and then to the neo-Gothic 19th-century bell tower next door. The church, which stands modestly to the right of the bell tower, is almost overlooked.

But of all the structures around the place du Louvre, the Eglise Saint-Germain-l'Auxerrois is the most venerable. Its history can be traced back to the 5th century, when an oratory was founded here to commemorate the passage of Germain, Bishop of Auxerre, through Paris on his way to Britain to evangelize the population there. The oratory was later transformed into a baptistery, and in the 11th century, King Robert the Pious transformed the baptistery into a church.

Sometime after the construction of the nearby Louvre fortress in 1200, Saint-Germain-l'Auxerrois became a royal parish. King Philippe II Auguste (founder of the Louvre) prayed in the church before the Battle of Bouvines in 1214, and returned there afterward to give thanks to God for his victory. King Charles V decided to make the Louvre a royal residence around 1380, and the proximity of this residence meant that the church would be associated with the great events of the realm. Processions and ceremonies required that it be lavishly decorated and furnished. During the reign of King Louis XIV, for example, it was hung with great tapestries representing the life of Saint Vincent for the ceremonies of *Fête-Dieu* (Feast of Corpus Christi).

The church that exists today is the result of the rebuilding of the one that Robert the Pious constructed. The choir, apse, and portals were built in the 13th century, the nave in the 14th century, the porch in the 15th century, and the chapels in the 16th century. Sadly, the 18th and 19th centuries brought irreparable destruction to the edifice, both for shortsighted reasons of "modernization" (for example, the destruction of a rood screen designed by Jean Goujon, under the pretext that the screen prevented the faithful from following the service taking place in the choir) and for political reasons (for example, the anti-royalist rampage of February 14, 1831).

The foundation of the bell tower that rises above the transept is the oldest part of this place of worship. It was part of the structure that Robert the Pious built in the 11th century, making Saint-Germain-l'Auxerrois one of the oldest churches in Paris. On the night of August 23, 1572, the bells in the tower rang to signal *matines* (night office of the canonical hours). Conspirators used the signal to begin their coordinated efforts to slaughter French Protestants in the early morning of August 24, an event that became known as the Saint Bartholomew's Day Massacre.

The flamboyant Gothic façade of the porch of the church is composed of five pointed arches, each with sculpted tracery. A menagerie of animals and human figures scamper here: a monkey with a bagpipe; a group of fighting dogs; a small, sleeping human figure; a menacing dragon. Flanking the archways are piers supporting statues of saints and other notables. Saint Mary of Egypt is represented here, dressed only in her long hair, and carrying the three loves of bread that would sustain her during her forty-seven years of penance in the desert. The original 15th-century statue of her stands inside, in the Chapel of the Virgin.

Several other statues of personages relevant to the history of Paris are represented on the portico. Saint Denis stands at one of the pillars, holding his decapitated head. He had been sent to Paris to spread the gospel in the 3rd century, but was arrested by the Romans and martyred.

In the embrasures to the right of the central doorway stand three figures. The one in the middle is Saint Genevieve, patron saint of Paris. She is particularly venerated for having prevented, through her prayers, an attack on the city by the forces of Attila the Hun. The 5th-century Germain of Auxerre met with Geneviève in Paris while on his way back from England; the abovementioned oratory erected on this spot marked this event.

Despite the destruction that the church has endured over the centuries, a number of splendid furnishings have been preserved. Enter to view a magnificent royal pew surmounted by a sculpted wooden canopy, a composition designed for King Louis XIV by renowned artist Charles Le Brun. The pew stands on the left-hand side of the nave, across from the pulpit, also by Le Brun. Another remarkable work is found in the chapel behind the pew—it is a 16th-century Flemish altarpiece in sculpted wood, displaying the Tree of Jesse and scenes from the life of Christ.

On the other side of the church (to the right upon entry), the Chapel of the Virgin provides a quiet place to repose and meditate. A second representation of the Tree of Jesse, this one designed by Viollet-le-Duc in the 19th century, stands at the end of this chapel.

The choir is enclosed by a polished wrought-iron-and-copper gate, installed by metalworker and locksmith Pierre Deumier in 1767. Saved from destruction at the time of the French Revolution, it was damaged during a ransack of the church in 1831.

The grand organ case in the gallery above the entryway was designed by Pierre-Noël Rousset. The organ itself, built by François-Henri Clicquot around 1771, had originally been installed at Sainte-Chapelle on Ile-de-la-Cité. The organ and case were transferred here in 1791 and fortunately escaped damage during the French Revolution.

To repair damage caused by the pillaging of the church in 1831, a number of architects undertook extensive restorations from 1838 to 1855. Among them was Victor Baltard, architect of the Baltard pavilions of Les Halles.

Just as Eglise Saint-German-l'Auxerrois has been greatly affected by the passage of time and by historical events, so has the area surrounding it. During the 9th century, plundering Norsemen seized the church and turned it into a fortress. The shape of the moat that they dug around the church can be seen today in the curve that is formed by the nearby rue Perrault. This street was once called Fossés-Saint-Germain-l'Auxerrois, referring to the *fossés*, or ditches. When the Norse were finally evicted from the church, they sacked and burned it, as well as the surrounding neighborhood.

During the great urbanization projects of the 19th century, the quarter was stripped of its narrow streets, and the space between the Colonnade du Louvre and the church was turned into a great square with a wide boulevard running through. Because of these transformations, many historical reference points have been irretrievably lost. The modern traveler, however, can enter the church and, in a few moments of reflection and with a bit of imagination, regain a sense of what life might have been like back in the times when France was a great kingdom, and Saint-Germain-l'Auxerrois was a royal parish church.

Tasty Treats

Dining In Paris
(2000)

Americans traveling to Paris may find dining a somewhat different experience from what they are accustomed to in the United States. For the French, dining is still generally a leisurely activity that is to be enjoyed for its own sake.

The following scenario illustrates what a customer dining in a restaurant in Paris is likely to experience.

We begin with the customer's arrival and reception by the headwaiter. Once seated, the customer is handed a menu and asked if he would like to be served an *apéritif* (before-dinner drink). The waiter then slips away to allow the customer to study the menu. In upscale restaurants, complementary *amuse-bouches*, bite-sized savories that whet the appetite, are often served at this time.

Next, the customer declares his order: first the *entrée* (starter), then the *plat principal* (main course). The dessert is not ordered at this time, unless it requires special preparation. The waiter then asks which wine the customer would like to select to accompany the meal. If the customer is unsure of how a particular wine would harmonize with the food, the waiter gives suggestions.

The waiter often proposes bottled mineral water (still or sparkling), but the customer may request a carafe of ordinary tap water. In either case, water is normally served chilled without ice.

After the waiter takes the order, he/she returns a few minutes later with the wine, opens the bottle, and offers it for tasting. Following the tasting ceremony, the server leaves the customer to enjoy conversation with his friends at the table. A few minutes later the *entrée* is served; the customer savors this course while continuing to engage in conversation with his companions. Once the *entrée* has been consumed, the waiter returns to clear the plates and utensils, replacing the knives and forks with clean ones.

The waiter then serves the *plat principal*. The customer and his friends relish every bite, relaxing and enjoying good conversation. The waiter does not return frequently to ask, "Is everything okay?" or "Can I get you anything else?" This aspect of service can be overdone in the US, whereas in France, the customer and his friends are left alone to enjoy their meal.

Following the *plat principal*, the waiter returns to take the dessert order. After this is served and consumed, he/she returns to propose a *café* (espresso). In upscale restaurants, a tray of chocolate truffles, mini-madeleines, or other sweets is often served with the coffee. Again, these are complementary. Following coffee the waiter may propose a *digestif* (after-dinner drink).

After dinner, the server does not clear away the water glasses or the coffee cups to leave the customers facing a naked table. Nor does he/she return with the bill until asked. This allows customers to relax and digest a good meal. When the customer finally leaves the table (usually two or three hours after his arrival), the headwaiter bids him farewell.

⁊   ℭ

As of 1 January 2008, all eating establishments in France are nonsmoking.

A Taste of Honey
(2003)

Paris is abuzz with bees! With honeybees, to be exact. And these honeybees actually produce—you guessed it—HONEY!

Far-fetched, you say? Not at all. When the Industrial Revolution brought country folk to Paris in droves, they did not turn into city people overnight. They brought their country ways with them, including their dining habits. They were able to buy fresh eggs, vegetables, and honey from nearby farmers, and were also able to buy honey in the city from convents and hospitals that kept their own hives. The name of a private apiary in the 5th *arrondissement*, the Rucher aux Sœurs (the Nuns' Apiary), recalls this bit of gastronomic history.

In 1856, the Paris government gave permission to one Henri Harnet to establish an apiary in the Jardin du Luxembourg. He was given space for twenty hives, and there he taught interested pupils the craft of beekeeping. This apiary still exists today, having been refurbished in 1991. There are numerous models of hives on display, the most original of which is a viola that the bees transformed into a home. The bees produce their honey from the flowers of the prolific apple and pear trees that grow in the garden not far from their hives. Classes in beekeeping and tree cultivation are made available to the general public by a nonprofit organization called the Société Centrale d'Apiculture (Central Apiculture Society). Each autumn they hold an open house, and the honey produced by the bees is sold.

Apiaries can be found in other parks and gardens around Paris and in neighboring suburbs. The one in Parc Kellerman (13th *arrondissement* near the Butte aux Cailles) consists of six colonies, two of which are housed in transparent hives to make their activities visible to visiting groups of children, and less frequently, adults. Founded in 1998, this apiary is maintained by the nonprofit group called L'Abeille Parisienne (The Paris Bee). In the 15th *arrondissement*, the apiary in the Parc Georges Brassens has introduced well over 35,000 students to the subject of beekeeping.

In a national park located in nearby Saint-Cloud, the Société Centrale d'Apiculture is responsible for the maintenance of the circular apiary located near

Luxembourg Garden apiary

the site of an old slaughterhouse, while in the Bois de Vincennes, the Syndicat National d'Apiculture (National Apiculture Syndicate) teaches beekeeping courses. In the town of Garches, a up of railway workers keeps several hives and sells their yield of honey annually.

The most curious and probably best-known apiary in Paris is the one located on the roof of the Palais Garnier, the old opera house in the 9th *arrondissement*. Its keeper, Jean Paucton, learned beekeeping in the Valensole region of France (famous for its lavender), and continued his education by taking classes in Paris. He bought his first swarm of bees in 1985, and installed them on the roof at Opéra, never imagining that they would produce honey. But after only one week, the hive was intensely active and honey was being produced. So Paucton established three additional hives there, each of which supports 20,000 to 30,000 bees. He eventually placed two on the roof of Paris' newest opera house at place de la Bastille as well.

Contrary to what you might think, the honey that these bees produce is of excellent quality. The bees gather pollen from the flora within a three-kilometer radius, including the gardens at Palais-Royal and Père Lachaise cemetery. Paucton's honey is sold in the boutiques at the Opéra as well as at Fauchon, one of Paris' most exclusive fine grocers.

There are a few boutiques that specialize in honeys, pollens, and other apiculture products. One of the most interesting is run by Jean-Jacques Schokmundés, head of L'Abeille Parisienne and motivating force behind the Parc Kellerman apiary. His shop is called Les Abeilles, and in it he sells pastries, jams and jellies, preserves, and mustards, as well as honey. Les Abeilles is located in the Butte aux Cailles quarter of the 13th *arrondissement*, not far from his beloved hives.

The oldest boutique is La Maison du Miel (9th *arrondissement*), founded in 1898. It moved to its present location on rue Vignon in 1905. The Galland family proudly offers over thirty varieties of honey to its customers, all of which you can taste prior to purchase. Honeys from the French provinces share shelf space with varieties from Canada, Turkey, Corsica, and other lands. And if you care to learn about the biological effects of various honeys, the Maison de Miel is the place for you—the Gallands can advise you on which types facilitate digestion (thyme), calm frazzled nerves (orange), stimulate the circulation (chestnut), and more.

Au Rucher de France is operated by the Syndicat National d'Apiculture (mentioned above). On the corner of rue de Rome and rue de Naples in the 8th *arrondissement*, it proudly proclaims to have everything required for apiculture as well as a variety of products from the hive.

For a taste of honey, Paris is the place to "bee"!

Les Abeilles
21, rue de la Buttes aux Cailles
75013 Paris
Tel: 01.45.81.43.48
Metro: Place d'Italie, Corvisart

La Maison du Miel
24, rue Vignon
75009 Paris
Tel: 01.47.42.26.70
Metro: Madeleine

Teatime in Paris
(2003)

In Paris, where cafés and coffee abound, where can a confirmed tea drinker find solace? At one of several *salons de thé* and/or unique tea vendors that compose a little known subset of the gastronomic enterprises here.

The city boasts several tearooms, ranging from the quiet, well-appointed Pegoty, which is not far from the Eiffel Tower in the 7th *arrondissement*, to the upscale Bernardaud on rue Royale between place de la Concorde and La Madeleine. Those that are true *salons de thé* will have a well-chosen variety of teas to propose, and will have a "teatime" that begins once the lunch crowd has deserted the restaurant.

Your tea-tasting experience can be as simple or as full of fanfare as you like. Pegoty offers a cozy "English Tea Time," with a copious tea service of dainty sandwiches, scones, and an assortment of tarts that can easily serve as a meal. Meanwhile, on the other side of the river, the four-star Bristol Hotel offers high tea with all the flourish of the Ritz in London—and throws in a designer fashion show on Saturday afternoons for good measure! If you have a taste for the exotic, then try the Mosquée on rue Geoffroy Saint-Hilaire, which whisks you away to the Maghreb, or Tch'a on rue du Pont-de-Lodi, which ushers you immediately to China. But for what may be the most extraordinary "French" tea experience in Paris, you must pay a visit to Mariage Frères.

Mariage Frères has three locations in Paris, the original of which is on the rue du Bourg-Tibourg in the Marais. The company has woven a beautiful tale from the family's 149-year history in the business (yes, the Mariage brothers really existed!), and the wonders and benefits of tea consumption. Each boutique/restaurant has its own "tea museum," a small collection of artifacts from the colonial days of importation from the Far East. Indeed, the museum at Bourg-Tibourg cites the ports for the company's first tea route in 1854–55 as Shanghai, Foochow, Amoy, Hong Kong, Whampoa, Canton, Macao, and Le Havre.

The Mariage Frère restaurants offer full service for lunch and brunch on weekends. But they also offer a bona fide teatime (3:00 p.m. to 6:30 p.m.), when you can sample sandwiches on bread made with Matcha tea, and a beautiful array of

La Maison des Trois Thés

Weighing tea

scones and pastries, some of which also contain tea as an ingredient. Whether you are simply taking tea or ordering a full meal, you are given a copy of a book entitled *L'Art Français du Thé* (*The French Art of Tea*), written by Mariage Frères and available in English to help you select your tea. The company has invented this concept of a French tea culture, of which the majority of the country seems to be ignorant. But it matters little, for once you are caught in the spell cast by the ambiance of this establishment, you are willing to believe almost anything they say with regard to tea!

Mariage Frères is also a bulk-tea vendor and a purveyor of all manner of packaged teas, accessories, and other objects relating to tea. Five hundred varieties of tea are stocked in canisters along the walls, and you are free to question the clerks about what type(s) of tea you wish to purchase. You are allowed to sniff the canister containing the tea that you are considering prior to making your final decision to purchase (much as you would take a whiff from the first glass of wine poured at your restaurant table before deciding whether or not to accept the bottle). When you have chosen your tea, you are given a ticket and asked to pay at the cash-register booth. You then return to your vendor, who weighs your tea and packages it for you.

This company has set the standard for vendors throughout France, and many others have either copied or slightly altered the Mariage Frères formula for promoting tea.

Le Palais des Thés (rue Vielle du Temple in the Marais) provides a unique tea-purchasing experience. Whereas Mariage Frères is decorated with dark wood and green plants to evoke the colonial past, the decor of Le Palais des Thés is conceived to impart a feeling of calm, of Zen. Soft music greets you as you enter the boutique, which is light, open, and airy. The accents of color come from the teapots and other accessories that lie on a few shelves, many of which are at or below eye level.

You are encouraged to smell different teas prior to making a purchase—a number of small glass jars covered with a piece of heavy frosted glass (reminiscent of the top of a perfume vial) contain samples of tea, and a small card provides information on the notes that you should be able to detect in them. The 100-gram, hermetically sealed packages of tea lie on the shelf immediately behind the jars containing the samples, so you cannot fail to locate the tea that you desire.

The company even provides free samples of tea to taste while you peruse the merchandise. A large container of tea can be found in the front and back rooms of the boutique, and Styrofoam cups are placed at your disposal so that you can sip the varieties that are being featured on any given day. A glass container next to the dispenser contains the tea leaves, and an adjacent card cites the pertinent information about the tea you are sampling. The back room contains the bulk teas to be weighed and sold, as well as pre-measured packets of organic teas. The store's personnel are friendly and helpful, making the entire experience a very pleasant one.

For the ultimate tea tasting experience in Paris, you should visit the inauspicious rue Gracieuse in the 5th *arrondissement*. There, you will find La Maison des Trois Thés—an unmarked, mysterious-looking place on the outside, and a treasure trove of teas and information about tea inside.

La Maison des Trois Thés is owned by Taiwanese tea master Madame Yu Hui Tseng, one of ten leading tea experts in the world, and the only woman in this class. Her business, as explained by her able French associate Fabien Maïolino, is primarily the cultivation and manufacture of tea. Her product is so well sought that she never has to worry about surplus stock. She specializes in the Oolong teas of Taiwan, selling over 99 percent of her stock to professionals. Upon entering her establishment, this quickly becomes apparent.

There is no tea odor emanating from the beautiful canisters perched upon their shelves high on the walls—if there were, this would mean that the teas were exposed to excess air and would be in the process of losing their aromas and flavors. The contents of the canisters are changed daily, ensuring that the freshest possible product is always available. Smoking and the wearing of perfume are strictly forbidden so that no strong odors can penetrate the teas. The staff will tell you that the basement houses a tea "cave," where over 1,000 varieties of tea are stored under controlled conditions. The water that is used for tea tasting is rigorously prepared to optimize the quality of the brewed liquid.

To the left of the entrance is a small area reserved for the general public. The Chinese tradition of *Gong Fu Cha* is presented here. Dating from the Ming Dynasty, this ceremony is designed to maximize the tea drinker's appreciation of the complexities of tea and to allow for multiple infusions of a single quantity of leaves. A server brings the water, the tea, and the accoutrements to your table, and instructs you on how to perform the ceremony. For subsequent infusions, you perform it yourself. No food is served here—the focus is solely on tea.

Monsieur Maïolino comes over from time to time to respond to questions and to share his passion for this ancient beverage with you. One of the things he emphasizes is that people who know and love wine are certain to appreciate tea. All of the reflexes developed and used by wine connoisseurs are those that are required to become a connoisseur of tea.

So tea drinkers in Paris need not despair. In fact, you may well consider that you are in a tea-lover's paradise!

Mariage Frères
30, rue du Bourg-Tibourg
75004 Paris
Tel: 01.42.72.28.11
Metro: Hôtel de Ville

Le Palais des Thés
64, rue Vielle du Temple
75003 Paris
Tel: 01.48.87.80.60
Metro: Saint-Sébastien Froissart, Filles de Calvaire

La Maison des Trois Thés
1, rue Saint-Medard (entrance on rue Gracieuse)
75005 Paris
Tel: 01.43.36.93.84
Metro: Place Monge

80   03

The tearooms Pegoty and Bernardaud are now closed.

Summer Strawberries
(2004)

What would summer in Paris be without strawberries? When this succulent, sweet, bright-to-deep red fruit appears in the markets, Parisians celebrate the coming of longer days, sunny skies, and the promise of slipping away for three to four weeks to the beach or to the French countryside.

While local markets almost always sell strawberries from Spain or Belgium, it is the French strawberries that one should watch for. Imported strawberries are often mass-produced, meaning they are likely to have been picked before ripening, and therefore are often tasteless and pulpy despite their rich color. But certain coveted French strawberries are virtually guaranteed to have been vine-ripened so as to develop full flavor and vitamin content prior to picking.

The earliest of these to arrive at the market is the Gariguette. It is grown in the Southwest region of France and brought to market in April and May. One of several products resulting from French breeding programs for strawberries, it is conical in shape and bursting with flavor. The Gariguette is classified as *nonremontante*, which means that the plants yield fruit only once each year. Thus its growing season is short, making its appearance on the market brief and its price expensive.

The Mara des bois strawberry is another French creation. It is well appreciated by growers because each plant produces many berries—reportedly as much as one kilogram per foot of ground planted. The strawberries are relatively small and have the flavor of *fraises des bois* (wild strawberries) that is so appreciated in France. They are fragile, but sweet and juicy. The Mara des bois is *remontante*, meaning that it continues to produce fruit from May through the first frost. It is, perhaps, the perfect strawberry!

The French have enjoyed cultivated strawberries since the Middle Ages, when they were first introduced into kitchen gardens. These were *fraises des bois* that were improved through experimentation with various planting techniques and fertilizers. Charles V ordered that wild strawberries be transplanted from the woods to the gardens of the Louvre in 1365. Centuries later, Louis XIV enjoyed strawberries grown at Versailles by the royal gardener La Quintinie.

Gariguettes   *Mara des Bois*

Even today, *fraises des bois* come in two varieties: truly wild or cultivated. Those that are wild are harvested in June and July in the plains, and in August and September in the mountains. The plants bear very small berries, but the fruit is a beautiful deep red and strongly perfumed. Cultivated *fraises des bois* are larger than wild ones; they are also less intensely colored and less fragrant. But compared to "regular" strawberries, they are still quite small (approximately one-half inch long) and perfumed. Both types of *fraises des bois* are quite fragile, and should be consumed immediately after purchase.

The large strawberries that Parisians enjoy today are descended from berries that were introduced to France by a sea captain named Frézier in 1713. Frézier transported strawberry plants from Chile to his home village of Plougastel in Brittany. There, he crossed them with North American strawberries to produce a plant that was the forerunner of today's strawberry. The plant, called a *fraisier*, was named after him.

The town of Plougastel was the strawberry-producing "capital" of France until World War II. In 1995, its local museum housed a five-room exhibit on the history of the strawberry in France. In 1997, the museum expanded the exhibit, adding a second floor of exhibition space and a documentation center devoted to strawberries. It has been renamed Musée de la Fraise et du Patrimoine (the Strawberry and Heritage Museum).

The strawberry is not truly a fruit, but rather the bulbous receptacle of the flower. The true fruit consists of the tiny grains that cover its surface. The plant is a member of the rose family; its Latin name *Fragaria* means "fragrant." The French have traditionally held it in high esteem, from the 13th century when it was thought that the plant had curative properties, through the 18th century when the berries were served to newlyweds as an aphrodisiac. Today, the strawberry remains the most popular fruit in France.

In the summer, Paris *pâtisseries* sell tarts studded with strawberries, as well as the famous strawberry, cream, and cake confection called the *frasier*. Strawberries are also featured on the dessert menus of the most humble to the most sophisticated restaurants, and are often served with a small dab of *crème chantilly* or a crispy thin *tuile* (butter cookie). The fruit is so esteemed for its inherent qualities that no additional garnish is considered necessary. And thanks to Gilles Marchal, *chef pâtissier* at the Hôtel Bristol in Paris, the strawberry is now used as an ingredient in savory dishes. Marchal proposes unusual, tempting recipes such as strawberry gazpacho with thyme and cucumber, and strawberry sandwiches, to stand alongside more traditional recipes. His first cookbook, devoted exclusively to the strawberry, is simply entitled *Fraise*.

Summer strawberries—just one more delight to experience in this beautiful city called Paris!

ဆ   ဣ

Gilles Marchal is now Creative Director at La Maison du Chocolat.

Macaron-festooned cakes

The Macaron—A Mouthful of Heaven
(2001)

If you love sweets, then on your next trip to Paris, look in pastry shops for the round, two-layered, pastel-colored pastries slightly reminiscent of hamburger buns. They appear almost artificial next to the luscious fruit tarts and multi-layered cream-and-chocolate confections in the shop windows. The uninitiated might even think that they were created specifically for children, so fanciful are their pink, green, and yellow hues. These pastries are called *macarons*, and despite their appearance, they are heavenly in both flavor and texture.

France is indebted to Italy for its introduction to this delicate pastry. It is widely believed that the Venetians discovered the *macaron* during their seafaring voyages of the Renaissance era, and that the chefs of Catherine de Medici brought the recipe to France at the time of Catherine's marriage to Henri II. The term *"macaron"* has the same origin as that of the word "macaroni"—both mean "fine dough."

The first *macarons* were simple cookies, made from almond powder, sugar, and egg whites. Many towns throughout France have their own prized tale surrounding this dessert. In Nancy, the granddaughter of Catherine de Medici was supposedly saved from starvation by eating them. In Saint-Jean-de-Luz, the *macarons* of Chef Adam regaled Louis XIV and Marie-Thérèse at their wedding celebration in 1660.

It was only at the beginning of the 20th century that the *macaron* became a "double-decker" affair. Pierre Desfontaines, owner of the famous Ladurée *pâtisserie* in Paris, got the idea of placing a layer of cream between two single *macaron* cookies while on a trip to Switzerland. *Macarons* in the form of a cream-filled pastry are now commonly found in *pâtisseries* throughout Paris, in flavors as standard as vanilla, chocolate, and coffee to those as exotic as rose and tea. But purists can still find the original almond-flavored pastries in food shops around town.

To determine who makes the best *macarons* in Paris, two members of our staff happily undertook the task of sampling the sweets around the city. We used Ladurée as the gold standard in this quasi-scientific yet taste bud-titillating survey of the *macarons* produced by five pastry shops in Paris.

A brief description of what we consider to be a good *macaron* is necessary in order to establish the ground rules under which we made this investigation. A good *macaron* should have a light, thin crust that gives way to a soft, chewy cookie that is also light and airy. The cream filling should have the same flavor as the cookie, should be thick but not pasty, and should offer an obvious contrast to the texture of the cookie. If these criteria are met, then the differentiating factor among good *macarons* is the quality of the flavorings used.

Weight, diameter, texture, and of course, flavor, were compared among the *macarons* of several *pâtisseries*. The one flavor that all the shops had in common was chocolate, so we paid special attention to that particular flavor for this taste test. With one exception, all the *macarons* tasted were three inches in diameter.

The Ladurée chocolate *macaron*, weighing in at 74 grams (19 FF each), had all of the qualities of a good *macaron* as described above. But one of our staff found the chocolate cream to have a smoky flavor that was slightly overpowering. Still, the overall score for this *macaron* was 8 out of a total of 10 points.

J. Y. Malitourne, in the 7th *arrondissement*, sells several kinds of chocolate *macarons*—regular chocolate (which we tasted), bitter chocolate, chocolate with bitter orange, chocolate with sea salt, and chocolate with pear and walnut. The regular chocolate *macaron* was the most disappointing we tasted at any of the *pâtisseries* we chose to evaluate. It weighed 72 grams, and cost 15 FF. The cookie was floury and the chocolate filling too dense. We gave it a 3/10.

At the acclaimed Maison Kayser of the 5th *arrondissement*, the dense cream filling of their chocolate *macaron* is made with dark chocolate. The cookie is also dense, so much so that it is almost indistinguishable from the cream center. A light, tender crust holds everything together. We gave this *macaron* (70 grams, 21 FF each) a score of 6/10.

On the other side of the Montagne Sainte-Geneviève on rue Mouffetard (5th *arrondissement*), Le Pâtissier du Marché offers a 3¼-inch chocolate *macaron* more dense than that offered by Ladurée—the cream is thicker, darker, and sweeter. The weight of the pastry (78 grams) corroborates this qualitative assessment. This *macaron* got a score of 7.5/10 (12 FF each).

The final "contestant" in our *macaron* contest was the chocolate *macaron* sold at the Grande Epicérie de Paris in the 7th *arrondissement*. The thickness of the cookie was approximately equal to that of the cream. The flavor of both the cookie and the cream was light, and the crust was especially light and tender. Weighing in at 74 grams and priced at 13,50 FF each, this *macaron* earned a score of 9/10.

La Grande Epicérie takes the prize for the best chocolate *macaron* sampled in our survey!

La Grande Epicérie
38, rue de Sèvres
75007 Paris
Tel: 01.44.39.81.00
Metro: Sèvres-Babylone

Ladurée
21, rue Bonaparte
75006 Paris
Tel: 01.44.07.64.87
Metro: St-Germain-des-Prés

℧   ℞

The pâtissier J. Y. Malitourne is now located in the 16th arrondissement.
Le Pâtissier du Marché in the 5th arrondissement is now closed.

Warming the Heart with Hot Chocolate
(2005)

Valentine's Day is the focal point for February's midwinter merriment, and with this celebration comes a renewed interest in chocolate. While most of us traditionally think of sweets when we want to give something special to that special someone, Discover Paris!™ suggests that it can be just as romantic to huddle and cuddle over an exceptional pot of hot chocolate. We present some of our favorite places for *chocolat chaud* below.

La Charlotte de L'Isle, on the Ile Saint-Louis, is a curious combination of children's theater, chocolate shop, and tea salon. Proprietor Sylvie Langlet has provided puppet shows, molded chocolates, and a wide variety of teas in this tiny shop for thirty years. The salon's two small rooms are pleasantly and whimsically cluttered; the disorder and an upright piano in the front room give the impression that you are visiting the home of an eccentric aunt. The establishment is entirely nonsmoking.

As for the hot chocolate, it is a connoisseur's dream! If you can imagine drinking a melted chocolate bar, you will have a good idea of what your experience at La Charlotte de L'Isle will be. Mme Langlet's hot chocolate is made with milk, but only enough to allow the mixture to liquefy. Dark, smooth, and unctuous, the chocolate coats the petite ceramic cups in which it is served. A pitcher of chocolate, cups, and a serving of water (presented in a chiseled carafe) are brought to the table on a tray from which you serve yourself. No additional milk is provided to dilute the chocolate—so if you prefer a thin version of this brew, La Charlotte may not be the place for you.

After this treat, if you would really like to indulge yourself and your sweetheart further, peruse Mme Langlet's selection of homemade chocolates, and purchase some to take home. Truffles, candied orange peel coated in dark chocolate, solid dark-chocolate mice, piglets, swans, and other fanciful creatures are displayed in the storefront window.

Le Rostand, on place Edmond Rostand in the 6th *arrondissement*, takes a different approach to its hot chocolate. You receive a traditional cup with a dose of chocolate syrup in the bottom. The walls of the cup have been "painted" with the chocolate so that the cup resembles a chocolate tulip. A pitcher of steamed milk is presented alongside, and you pour as much or as little of it as you like into your chocolate. Stir and you have a rich, smooth hot chocolate, made to order. The chocolate is flavored with a small amount of vanilla, as witnessed by the grains of vanilla bean that you will find in your cup after you have finished savoring your beverage.

The only potential disadvantage with this method of serving hot chocolate is that you are served a greater volume of milk than chocolate. If you like potent hot chocolate, you end up with lots of milk left over. If you are an aficionado of steamed milk, however, you will likely be quite happy.

Le Rostand's sidewalk terrace offers a splendid view of the Luxembourg Garden, the comings and goings of people from all walks of life, and the photographic exhibits sponsored by the Sénat that are displayed on the garden's wrought-iron gates. In the winter, the heated terrace is enclosed and divided by thick, clear plastic sheets. Half of it is designated as nonsmoking.

If you are interested in purchasing chocolate bonbons after your hot chocolate experience at Le Rostand, just pop over to **Dalloyau**, two doors away on place Edmond Rostand. This boutique is part of the Dalloyau chain of gourmet shops founded in 1802. Dalloyau sells roughly fifty-five tons of chocolate at its various outlets each year.

Over on the Right Bank, two establishments are "absolute musts" for chocoholics. **Angelina**, facing the Tuileries Garden on rue de Rivoli, is a venerable institution. Its famous "Chocolat Africain" is perhaps the thickest and richest in the city. The service is traditional—a pitcher of chocolate and cups inscribed with "Angelina"; stemmed glasses, each with a single ice cube; a pitcher of water, and a small mountain of *crème chantilly* are brought to your table. The chocolate is dark, but surprisingly sweet. Because of the sweetness, we found the water to be a welcome part of the service. With a generous dollop of whipped cream mixed into your cup, you can easily imagine that you are drinking warmed chocolate ice cream!

Nonsmokers can enjoy their chocolate in a dedicated area at the rear of the dining room. A small but eye-catching display of chocolates (including giant truffles) is located at the entry to the dining room, so it is possible to purchase a bit of chocolate heaven when you are ready to leave.

Jean-Paul Hévin, less than a five-minute walk from Angelina, is located on rue Saint-Honoré. Hévin has made a name for himself as one of the city's premier *chocolatiers*. On the ground floor, you find the boutique, which is slick and minimalist, and looks more like a jewelry store than a chocolate shop. Upstairs is the *salon de thé*, divided into two areas of roughly equal size for smokers and nonsmokers. The décor is similar to that of the boutique—dark, wood-grained walls are hung with beautiful photos of the confections that you can purchase downstairs. Brown tables and sturdy wicker chairs complete the interior design scheme that evokes chocolate and nuts. Classical music plays softly in the background as you contemplate the menu, which is replete with chocolate pastries.

Steaming hot chocolate is served in individual classic white porcelain pitchers and cups. A bowl of brown and white lumps of sugar is presented alongside, but water is not part of the service. The *chocolat chaud* is everything one would expect from a master chocolate maker—full bodied, rich, and very slightly sweet.

La Charlotte de L'Isle (our favorite)
24, rue Saint-Louis en l'Ile
75004 Paris
Tel: 01.43.54.25.83
Metro: Sully-Morland

ᘏ ᘒ

As of 1 January 2008, all eating establishments in France are nonsmoking.

Fresh-Roasted Coffee in Paris
(2007)

Tradition has it that coffee was introduced to Paris at the Saint-Germain fair in 1672, when a certain Armenian, Pascal Haroukian, opened a *maison de café* similar to those he had seen in Constantinople.

The fair has long ceased operation, but the custom of forming friendships, disputing political views, and "reinventing the world" around a cup of espresso continues to this day.

To learn about the art of roasting coffee—a crucial link between the growing of the bean and brewing it for drinking—we met with a local artisanal coffee roaster. Jean-Paul Logereau, a third-generation *torréfacteur* (coffee merchant), welcomed our interest in his profession, and willingly answered our questions about coffee roasting and brewing. It was a delight for us to step into his shop and to savor the aroma of freshly roasted coffee!

Logereau is proprietor of La Brûlerie des Gobelins, located at 2, avenue des Gobelins in the 5th *arrondissement*. His grandfather began his career in the coffee business in the city of Orleans. In the 1930s, the family moved to Paris, and the grandfather established a *brûlerie* (roasting facility) on boulevard Saint-Jacques. His two sons (Logereau's father and uncle) opened a second shop on rue de l'Estrapade, and Logereau worked there with them. The Estrapade site supplied restaurants and gourmet grocers such as Hédiard and Fauchon, and also operated as a café until 1978.

When the family decided to sell the business, Mr. Logereau went to work as a tea merchant for roughly five years before acquiring a *brûlerie* of his own. Located at the intersection of avenue des Gobelins and rue de Valence, the shop had been in existence as a roasting facility since 1945.

In the family tradition, Logereau continues to supply restaurants and *bistrots* with excellent coffees. His clients range from the modest to the upscale—examples include the simple, yet acclaimed, *bistrot* L'Oursin in the 13th *arrondissement*, and the exquisite restaurants at the luxury Hôtel Meurice. Having been in the coffee-roasting business for about forty-five years, Mr. Logereau's extensive network of contacts serves him well.

But Logereau says that the *raison d'être* for La Brûlerie des Gobelins is to attract and serve walk-in clients from the neighborhood. His shop is well placed for this, as it is located near the highly praised Le Boulanger de Monge, and less than a five-minute walk from rue Mouffetard, a street renowned for its outdoor markets and gourmet food shops.

Mr. Logereau roasts his coffees using a gas-fired Probat, a German-made machine. Although it will hold up to thirty kg at one time, he uses it for roasting beans in small batches of about two to five kg. Roasting takes place in a drum at temperatures around 210°C for a period of fifteen to twenty minutes, depending upon the type of bean and the degree of darkness that he wants to achieve. During the process, Logereau extracts samples of beans to determine their aroma and color. He also listens as the beans expand and crackle, a sign that they will soon be ready for release from the drum. When the time comes, he opens the door to the drum, allowing the roasted beans to spill onto a circular cooling tray. Blades turn the beans to aerate them uniformly as a fan beneath the tray forces air through them. When the beans are cool, he transfers them to a container and lets them sit overnight before selling them retail or delivering them to his restaurant clients. He believes that the process of letting the beans settle for a day allows their flavor to develop fully.

Logereau sells only Arabica coffees to his retail customers. He prefers Ethiopian coffees—Harrar, Sidamy, and Yrgasheffe—but he also sells varieties from Kenya, New Guinea, Haiti, Central and South America, and Indonesia. He offers six to seven different blends (beans from various locations that are mixed to achieve a balance of aroma and flavor), as well as unblended coffee. The blends are identified by name (Sienne or Venise, for example) and the unblended beans are sold under the name of their region or country of origin.

For his restaurant and hotel clients, Logereau creates blends according to their specifications. For example, some hotels require a Robusta blend because this type of coffee retains its flavor better over the course of the breakfast service. The more delicate Arabica must be served immediately, because it tends to caramelize and lose its flavor while being held in a heated container.

Mr. Logereau occasionally holds coffee tastings, especially when a new batch of beans arrives. Representatives from the embassies of Guatemala, Ethiopia, and Salvador have attended tastings that featured coffee from these countries.

According to Logereau, the preferred way to make a cup of coffee is with a *cafetière à piston*, known in English as the French press, press pot, or coffee plunger. This method captures the coffee's flavor and essential oils, and brings out the qualities of the brew better than any other method. He also likes coffee prepared by espresso machines, and considers the best apparatus to be a Swiss brand called Jura

(which, incidentally, he sells in his shop). This is a machine of solid construction, but the cost of around 1,000€ is beyond the reach of many consumers.

There are two other conventional methods of preparing coffee: using a coffee filter (of paper, or, preferably, of gold-plated mesh) for drip brewing, and using an Italian stovetop espresso maker (also called a moka pot). However, paper filters tend to absorb oils, removing flavor from the coffee, while the water temperature in stovetop espresso makers rises above 100°C (optimal water temperature is 82°C), and burns off much of the coffee's aroma.

Industry innovations have consistently eroded the retail client base of the artisanal *torréfacteur*. Many years ago, it was the advent of mass distribution of ground coffee in supermarkets. Now there is Nespresso, a machine that produces an excellent espresso from ground coffee that is packed in a small aluminum capsule. Additionally, there is Starbucks, which is now just as ubiquitous in Paris as McDonald's.

Logereau does not feel threatened by the competition occasioned by Nespresso or Starbucks. While he believes that his retail customers might be attracted to Nespresso, he notes that the capsules are expensive and that distribution is restricted to Nespresso stores. And he notes that clients who appreciate artisanally roasted coffees shun supermarket brands and the syrup-flavored brews that Starbucks has made famous.

If the number of clients we saw entering and leaving his boutique during the time that we spent there is any indication, then indeed Mr. Logereau has nothing to worry about. What keeps them coming back for his product is his knack for knowing just when to adjust the temperature in the drum, when the aroma, color, and volume of the beans are approaching perfection, and listening for the crackling of the beans that signals that he should stop the roasting process. In other words, it is the combination of his skills and artistic sensibilities that make his coffees so desirable.

La Brûlerie des Gobelins
2, avenue des Gobelins
75005 Paris
Tel: 01.43.31.90.13
Metro: Censier Daubenton, Gobelins

Wine Pairing for Your Christmas Feast
(2004)

Christmas is fast approaching, and markets all over Paris are stocking up on goose, turkey, and capon to grace holiday tables for the annual *reveillon*, or Christmas dinner. Some regions of France share with the US the tradition of eating turkey and stuffing as the main course, but for the remainder of the meal, there is little similarity between the dining customs of the two countries. *Foie gras*, oysters, and cheeses figure heavily in the Parisian repast, and the Yule log (*bûche de Noël*) is a favorite dessert in France. But perhaps the biggest difference between the culinary culture of Christmas dinner in France and the US is the French custom of selecting wines to accompany each course.

Recently touted as "wine pairing" in the US, this tradition has existed in France for centuries. And as Discover Paris!™ colleague and wine specialist Daniel says, "The wines served at the *reveillon* have to be the best ones of the year—it's a fest!"

Daniel describes himself as a "typically French" man who comes from a family of gourmets with a long tradition of seeking and finding the best wines that France has to offer. He is thoroughly familiar with France's wine-producing regions, their history, their best products, and the best places to purchase them in Paris. He also knows how to pair these wines with food, having begun his lessons over twenty-five years ago.

We asked Daniel to share some wine-pairing tips for Christmas dinner with our readers, and he was more than happy to comply. Here are his recommendations:

"Start with a good champagne! To appreciate the subtleties and finesse of brut champagne, it should be consumed as an *apéritif.* If you wish to consume champagne during the meal, choose a Blanc de Noirs—a vintage containing a high percentage of pinot noir grapes."

Entrée (Starter)

"Sweet wines like Sauternes, Vouvray *moëlleux,* or Coteaux du Layon are great accompaniments for *foie gras.* But if you prefer oysters, you should choose your wine according to the organoleptic characteristics of those oysters. For example, Bouzigues oysters from Languedoc-Roussillon are strongly iodated, and thus

require a strong white wine such as a Picpoul de Pinet (also from Languedoc-Roussillon). In contrast, Belon oysters from Bretagne have a delicate taste of almond and hazelnut—you will better appreciate a rather delicate wine like a white Burgundy or a Chablis Premier Cru from Burgundy Auxerrois with these. A good Muscadet or Gros Plant (Loire Valley), or a *petit* white Graves from Aquitaine will accompany hollow oysters such as Fines de Claire or Arcachon.

"If you have seafood such as lobster or crayfish, it's time to open a Montrachet or a Corton Charlemagne. A good Meursault Premier Cru or a Chablis Grand Cru would be fine as well."

Plat principal (Main course)

"Then comes the turkey! It would be interesting to try an old Meursault with this because the white flesh of the bird is very subtle and delicate. But if you don't want a white wine, try a burgundy like a Côtes de Beaune, Savigny les Beaune, Aloxe-Corton, or a Beaune Premier Cru; these wines are also very subtle, and elegant.

"If you have a goose with a fatter, brown flesh, it's better trying to counterbalance it with a more acidic red wine like a great Bordeaux—a red Bandol would do nicely.

"If you are fortunate enough to be serving truffles, think of a Pomerol, a Saint-Emilion, or a big northern Côtes du Rhone such as Côte-Rôtie or Ermitage.

"With game, such as wild duck, deer, or wild boar, the great Burgundies from Côtes de Nuits and Côtes de Beaune are required. These wines have dreamy names: Corton, Romanée, Nuits Saint-Georges, Chambertin, and so on."

Fromage (Cheese course)

"If you still have room for cheese, select white wine to accompany goat cheeses. For example, choose a Sancerre to accompany a Crottin de Chavignol. Sweet white wines (*vins doux naturels*) such as Maury or Rivesaltes are perfect for Roquefort or other blue cheeses. Select a *vin jaune* for a Comté, but choose cider for a good Camembert because they come from the same *terroir*."

Salade (Salad)

"Forego the wine with the salad course. Nothing but a glass of water is required."

Dessert

"Port, Maury, Rivesaltes, or Banyuls pair well with chocolate cake. But select a Sauternes for an orange tart or cake. Sweet wines from the Loire Valley are wonderful with apple cake. I recommend serving *bûche de Noël* with water, but if you really want to have wine with it, choose a sweet one like Maury or Porto to suit the flavor of the creamy filling of the cake (generally chocolate butter, pecan, hazelnut, or *praliné*). You can also try a *demi-sec* champagne or a small glass of an *eau de vie* such as *quetsche* or *mirabelle* (types of prunes) or *framboise* (raspberry).

"For a decadent finish to a lovely meal, but without the sweets, choose an Yquem and drink it by itself!

"But be sure not to drive after that!!!"

Paris, Past and Present

Vélib' station

Vélib'
(2007)

Since mid-July, Paris' public transportation system has undergone a revolution. The city has installed hundreds of bicycle rental stations throughout town and the phrase "Let a thousand flowers bloom" now describes the velocipede phenomenon. Having determined that most users make bicycle trips that take only twenty-five minutes, the city has designed a rental service to suit the transportation needs of these riders. The first thirty minutes are free, but if the bicycle is not returned to a rental station by the end of that period, charges start to accrue. Considering the cost of half-day or full-day rental, travelers who want to see Paris by bicycle would do well to rent one from a private concession. However, judging from the number of new pearl-gray bicycles that appeared on the streets on July 15th, and the increasing number of persons riding them, the service, called *Vélib'*, has already inspired Parisians to use a bicycle for short trips around town.

La Fontaine des Innocents

La Fontaine des Innocents

(2007)

When famed Italian sculptor Giovanni Lorenzo Bernini visited Paris in 1665, he declared upon viewing the Fontaine des Innocents that it was the most beautiful thing in Paris.

The fountain was built between 1547 and 1549, next to the Cemetery of the Holy Innocents on the corner of rue Saint-Denis and what is now rue Berger for the occasion of King Henri II's solemn entry into Paris. It was originally designed as a loggia (an elevated covered terrace) for persons of high rank to occupy during the royal procession. At the base of the loggia were six spigots that provided trickles of water for thirsty Parisians. It was, as one writer remarked, "A lot of architecture for so little water."

After the cemetery was closed in 1786, the fountain was moved to the center of the plaza. No longer serving as a loggia, it was redesigned so that water would gush out of an elevated water basin installed there. The most remarkable thing about the fountain, however, is not the gushing water but the sculpted nymphs that stand between the pilasters. Five of these were carved by Jean Goujon, one of the major figures of the French Renaissance. He is celebrated for the sensuality and fluidity of his sculpted figures, and these may well be "the most beautiful thing in Paris" to this day.

The Fearsome Dragon
of the Jardin des Plantes
(2007)

Guarding the north entrance of the Jardin des Plantes stands a dragon of realistic proportions, possessing scales of crushed aluminum cans, a body of cardboard, and flames of plastic—all from recycled materials. Comically ferocious, it attracts the attention of adults and children alike.

The sculpture was created for the exposition "Dragons," held from April 5– November 6, 2006 at the Muséum National d'Histoire Naturelle. It embodies not only the universal fascination for mythical beasts, but also the efforts of the city of Paris to encourage recycling.

ꝏ   ꞇ

The dragon has been removed from the garden.

La Guillotine
(2007)

Contrary to popular belief, Joseph-Ignace Guillotin did not invent the guillotine. The deadly machine had been used for executions in Italy at least since the 15th century. In France, the first record of its use was in 1632, for the execution of Henri de Montmorency, who had participated in a rebellion against Louis XIII.

Guillotin's intent in introducing a bill for the use of the device was to make capital punishment democratic and painless. Up until 1789, common criminals suffered execution by burning or worse, whereas only noblemen benefited from the quick death of the executioner's ax. Guillotin asserted that when the blade fell, the condemned would feel only a fresh sensation on his neck. While this declaration provoked laughter in the National Assembly, the body passed into law the use of the machine on January 21, 1790. The device quickly became the symbol of state repression (or Revolutionary justice, depending upon your point of view) during the period known as the Terror.

The guillotine in this photograph stands against a wall in the Le Caveau des Oubliettes. The barman there asserts that it is a genuine device and that it was used by the French army in the provinces to execute counterrevolutionaries in 1793.

Toni Morrison at the Louvre
(2007)

In November 2006, Nobel and Pulitzer Prize winner Toni Morrison presided over a special month-long program at the Louvre entitled *Etranger Chez Soi*. Using the Géricault painting *Raft of the Medusa* as a focal point of her opening conference, Morrison expounded upon this topic, which she translated into English as meaning both "The Foreigner's Home" (in the sense of possessing a home) and "The Foreigner is Home." Over the course of the month that followed, conferences, readings, and other events explored this theme as it relates not only to the plastic arts, but also to dance, film, and literature. Debates were held on whether or not museums should have a role in promoting cultural diversity and social integration. As an example of this notion, Géricault's *Raft of the Medusa* was used as a backdrop for a slam poetry session in which ten of Paris' best slammers expressed their opinions on the works of their choice.

Invited by the Louvre to serve as guest curator, Morrison worked with the museum for two years to present this series of events, which the *New York Times* described as "a multidisciplinary program on displacement, immigration, and exile." It was truly an extraordinary affair!

Oldest street sign in Paris

Oldest Street Sign
(2007)

Hundreds of years before it became the heart of the Latin Quarter, rue Galande constituted the beginning of a road that led up the north slope of Montagne-Sainte-Geneviève via rue Descartes, down the south side via rue Mouffetard, and then beyond to the city of Lyon. Today, in a nearby alleyway, one can see an immense slab of paving stone that attests to the existence of ancient Roman roads that once crisscrossed the city. The alleyway lies to the right of the Saint-Julien-le-Pauvre church, whose construction began in the 12th century.

And on rue Galande, one can see—dating from the 14th century—the oldest street sign in Paris. Carved in stone, it is a low relief of the mythical Saint-Julien-le-Pauvre and his wife conducting Christ across a river in a boat. The sign is a registered historic monument (I.S.M.H.—l'Inventaire Supplémentaire des Monuments Historiques).

Église Saint-Julien-le-Pauvre

Roman paving stone

About Discover Paris!™

About Discover Paris!™

Seventeen years ago, we relocated to Paris to experience a more slow-paced and culturally enriched lifestyle. As our love affair with the city grew with each passing year, our desire to share our knowledge of, and passion for, Paris grew as well. In 1999, we founded Discover Paris!™ to satisfy this desire to serve you, the Paris-bound traveler.

Discover Paris!™ clients are well educated, discriminating travelers who desire a richer and more in-depth experience in Paris than the average tourist does. Whether traveling alone, with a companion, with family, or with a small group, you want to know how to make Paris your own. You do not have the time—or do not want to spend the time—to research hotels, restaurants, or possible itineraries. Yet you want the assurance that the hotels, restaurants, and activities proposed to you will give you the utmost in satisfaction!

Discover Paris!™ is here to act as your eyes, ears, and legs in Paris, and to take the work out of your travel planning. You can therefore expect greater depth and attention to detail from our recommendations than from those found in guidebooks and on Web sites. Each hotel that we recommend has been personally investigated. Our staff has dined at the restaurants that we recommend, and each itinerary has been personally researched.

The depth of detail in our travel plans would be difficult for you to match without taking days or weeks of your valuable time selecting and reading guidebooks, contacting tourist offices, phoning abroad, and researching information on the Internet. And even if you chose to expend the time and energy to undertake this level of travel planning, you would not have the added benefit of the personal recommendations of our full-time Paris residents.

Discover Paris!™ focuses exclusively on Paris so that we can concentrate on bringing you the best and most current information on what the City of Light has to offer. Nothing is prepackaged; based on your responses to our travel planning questionnaire, we provide you with a truly personalized itinerary with which you can explore the facets of the city that are of particular interest to you.

Discover Paris!™ is here to help you make your next trip to Paris everything you want it to be. Why not allow yourself the luxury of our specialized services? Please visit our Web site: **www.discoverparis.net.**

Index

A

A l'heure de l'observatoire, les Amoureux • 43

A Moveable Feast • 29

Abeille, Parisienne, L' • 79, 81

Abeilles, Les • 81

Académie de la Grande Chaumière • 32

American Church in Paris • 35

Anderson, Margaret • 36

Anderson, Sherwood • 29

Angelina • 96

Anguier, Michel • 64

Anne of Austria • 61, 63, 64, 65

apéritif • 77, 103

apiary • 79–81

Arago medallions • 37

Arc de Triomphe • 1, 2, 69, 136

Arrosoir, L' • 58

Art Français du Thé, L' • 84

Artur, José • 15

Association Evangélique d'Eglises Baptistes de Langue Française, L' • 59

Atelier de Saint-Paul • 32

Ateliers de Beaux-Arts • 32

Attila the Hun • 72

avenue Daumesnil • 58

avenue de l'Ouest • 42

avenue des Champs-Elysées • 1–2, 13, 24, 69, 134

avenue des Gobelins • 99, 102

avenue Ledru Rollin • 58

B

baguettes • 24

Baigneuse, La • 31, 32, 134

bakery • 5, 19

Baltard pavilions • 73

Baltard, Victor • 73

bar • 5, 12, 13, 19, 20, 22, 43, 134

   Caveau des Oubliettes, Le • 22, 115

   Dingo Bar • 29

   Divan du Monde, Le • 22

   Feria Café • 20, 134

   Indiana Bar • 20, 134

   Jockey, The • 43

Barsotti, Jacqueline • 43

Bastille Day • 2, 136

bateaux mouches • xii, 4

Baudouin II • 53

Beach, Cyprian • 35

Beach, Eleanor • 35

Beach, Sylvester • 35

Beach, Sylvia • 30, 35–36

beekeeping • 79–80

Belleville • 39

Berger d'Israël • 58

Bernardaud • 83, 86

Bernini, Giovanni Lorenzo • 111

BHV (Bazar de l'Hôtel de Ville) • 8, 23

bicycle • 109

Bièvre • 9–11

Bioux, Les • 46

bistrot • 99

Black and White • 42

Bleustein-Blanchet, Marcel • 13

Bois de Vincennes • 80

boissonerie • 49

Bon Marché, Le • 20

Bordeaux • 46, 104

Boulanger de Monge, Le • 100

boulangerie • 19

boulevard du Montparnasse • 41, 43

boulevard Edgar Quinet • 42

boulevard Raspail • 42

boulevard Saint-Germain • 58

boulevard Saint-Jacques • 99

Bourbons of France • 61

brasserie • 12, 13, 14, 20, 30, 134

Broca, Henri • 43

Brown, Dan • 37

brûlerie • 99

Brûlerie des Gobelins, La • 99–102

bûche de Noël • 25, 103, 105

Buci market • 46

Bury, Pol • 136

Butte aux Cailles • 79, 81

Butte Chaumont • 1, 7

C

café • 2, 5, 6, 13, 14, 19, 20, 29, 39, 41, 42, 57, 58, 78, 99, 134
   Arrosoir, L' • 58
   Café de la Mairie • 134
   Café Marly • 57
   Closerie des Lilas, La • 28, 29, 134
   Dôme, Le • 29, 40, 41, 42, 43, 135
   Feria Café • 20, 134
   Indiana Bar • 20, 134
   Nemrod, Le • 19
   Rotonde, La • 40, 41, 135
   Starbucks • 6, 102
capon • 25, 103
Carpeaux, Jean-Baptiste • 136
carrefour Vavin • 41, 43
Carrousel • 136
Carrousel du Louvre • 37
Catholic Paris Web site • 59
Cavaillé-Coll, Aristide • 59, 69
Caveau des Oubliettes, Le • 22, 115
Cemetery of the Holy Innocents • 111
Central Apiculture Society • 79
Centre Pompidou • 43
Cézanne, Paul • 30
Chaillot • 1, 2
Chalgrin, Jean-François • 69
champagne • 103, 105, 134, 136
   Blanc de Noirs • 103
Champs-Elysées • 1–2, 13, 24, 69, 134
Chardin, Jean-Baptiste Simeon • 33
Charité, La • 58
Charles V • 71, 87
Charles X • 68
Charlotte de l'Isle, La • 95, 97, 136
Châtelet • 6
cheese • 24, 25, 103, 105
   Camembert • 105
   Comté • 105
   Crottin de Chavignol • 105

   Roquefort • 105
Chef Adam • 91
chocolat chaud • 95, 97
chocolate • 19, 25, 78, 91, 92, 93, 95–97, 105, 136
Choiselat, Louis-Isidore • 68
Christ • 23, 53, 64, 68, 72, 119
Christian • 38, 53, 57–59
Christmas • 23–25, 103, 134
cider • 105
Clicquot, François-Henri • 69, 73
Closerie des Lilas, La • 28, 29, 134
coffee • 6, 14, 20, 25, 78, 83, 91, 99–102, 136
Colonnade du Louvre • 71, 73
Comédie Française • 37
copyist • 31–33
Corot, Jean-Baptiste Camille • 33
Coupole, La • 43
Cour Napoléon • 37
Cowley, Malcolm • 29
crayfish • 104
crèche • 25
croissants • 19
Cross of Christ • 53
Crown of Thorns • 53
Cunard, Nancy • 43

D

Da Vinci Code, The • 37–39, 68
Dada • 41, 42, 43
Dadaism • 42
Dalloyau • 96
Daniel • 103
de Balzac, Honoré • 20
de Castelbajac, J. C. • 15
de Gaulle, Charles • 2
de Gergy, Languet • 68
de Medici, Catherine • 91
Delacroix, Eugène • 68
Dernière Goutte, La • 44, 45, 46, 47, 49, 135
Desfontaines, Pierre • 91
Desnos, Robert • 42
Deumier, Pierre • 73

Dingo Bar • 29

Discover Paris!™ • 25, 45, 95, 103, 123–124

Divand du Monde, Le • 22

dog • 5–8, 43

Dôme, Le • 29, 40, 41, 42, 43, 135

dragon • 72, 113, 135, 136

Drugstore Publicis • 13–15, 134

Duc, Le • 62, 64

Ducasse, Alain • 14, 15

Duchamp, Marcel • 41, 43

Duke of Anjou • 62

Dumas, Alexandre père • 20

E

Easter • 57, 68

Eastern Orthodox Church • 54

eau de vie • 105

   framboise • 105

   mirabelle • 105

   quetsche • 105

Ecole du Louvre • 32

Ecole Grégoire Ferrandi • 46

Eglise Baptiste • 57

Eglise Saint-Antoine des Quinze-Vingts • 56, 58, 135

Eglise Saint-Ephrem • 58, 135

Eglise Saint-Germain-l'Auxerrois • 70–73, 135

Eglise Saint-Jean-l'Evangéliste • 136

Eglise Saint-Julien-le-Pauvre • 119, 136

Eiffel Tower • 24, 25, 83, 136

espresso • 14, 19, 20, 48, 78, 99, 100, 102

Etoile de Mer, L' • 42

Etranger Chez Soi • 117

Evangelical Association of French-Language Baptist Churches • 59

Exaltation of the Holy Cross, The • 55

Exposition dada MAN RAY • 42

F

faubourg Saint-Jacques • 61

Fauchon • 81, 99

Fédération des Eglises Evangéliques Baptistes, La • 57

Federation of Evangelical Baptist Churches • 57

Feria Café • 20, 134

Ferris wheel • 1, 134

Figaro, Le • 48

Fish • 45, 47, 48, 49

Fitzgerald, F. Scott • 29

Flame of Remembrance • 2

foie gras • 14, 24, 103

Foire de Saint-Nicolas • 23

Fontaine des Innocents, La • 110–111, 136

Fort, Paul • 35

Fossés-Saint-Germain-l'Auxerrois • 73

Foujita, Tsuguharu • 41, 42

Fraise • 87–89

fraises des bois • 87–88

François I • 68

Franco-Prussian War • 2

French Art of Tea, The • 84

French press • 100

French Renaissance • 111

French Revolution • 53, 57, 64, 67, 73

Frézier (sea captain) • 88

G

Galland family • 81

Garches • 80

Gare d'Austerlitz • 9

Gariguette • 87–88, 135

Gauguin, Paul • 33

Géricault, Théodore • 33, 117

Germain, Bishop of Auxerre • 71

Gift, The • 42

Giovanna • 7, 8

gnomon • 37, 68

Gong Fu Cha • 85

goose • 25, 103, 104

Goujon, Jean • 71, 111

Grande Arche de la Défense • 1, 134

Grande Epicérie de Paris • 93

Grande Mosquée de Paris • 17–18

Guillotin, Joseph-Ignace • 115

guillotine • 115, 136

Guyancourt • 9

H

Habsburgs of Spain • 61
Halles, Les • 5, 73
hammam • 17–18
Harnet, Henri • 79
Haroukian, Pascal • 99
Hédiard • 99
Hemingway, Ernest • 29–30
Hemingway, Hadley • 29, 30
Henri de Montmorency • 115
Henri II • 91, 111
Henry, David P. • 37–39
Hermé, Pierre • 136
Hévin, Jean-Paul • 96
Holy Trinity • 65
honey • 79–81
hot chocolate • 95–97, 136
Hôtel Bristol • 83, 89
Hôtel de Ville • 23, 25, 86
Hôtel des Ecoles • 42
Hôtel Istria • 43
Hôtel Lenox • 42
Hôtel Meurice • 99

I

I.S.M.H. • 119
Ile Saint-Louis • 95, 134
Ile-de-la-Cité • 73
Indiana Bar • 20, 134
Ingres, Jean-Auguste-Dominique • 31, 33
internment camp • 36
Invalides • 1
Inventaire Supplémentaire des Monuments
    Historiques • 119

J

Jane • 5–6, 8, 31–33, 134
Jardin des Plantes • 113, 136
Jardin des Tuileries • 1
Jardin du Luxembourg • 7, 79
jazz • 22

Jefferson, Thomas • 2
Jennifer • 7, 8
Jimpy • 6, 7–8, 134
Jockey, The • 43
Joyce, James • 36

K

Kedroff Vocal Ensemble • 53, 54, 55
Kedroff, Alexandre • 53, 55
Kedroff, Nicolas • 55
Kiki • 41, 43

L

Ladurée • 91, 92, 93, 136
Langlet, Sylvie • 95
Latin Quarter • xii, 119
Lebrun, Albert • 36
Le Brun, Charles • 72
Le Duc, Gabriel • 62, 64
Le Muet, Pierre • 62, 64
Le Nôtre • 1
Lee, Baldwin • 38
Legion of Honor • 36
Lemercier, Jacques • 62
Lenin, Vladimir • 41
Lent • 53
Lezarts de la Bièvre • 9–11
Lezarts sur les Murs • 9–11
Liberation of Paris • 2
Liberty Guiding the People • 68
Librairie Six • 42
Lipp, Brasserie • 30
Little Review, The • 36
lobster • 14, 104
Logereau, Jean-Paul • 98–102, 136
Louis IX • 53, 58
Louis XIII • 61, 63, 115
Louis XIV • 61, 62, 71, 72, 87, 91
Louvre • 1, 19, 31, 32, 33, 37, 38, 68, 71, 73, 87,
    117, 134, 135, 136
Luxembourg garden • 7, 79, 80, 96, 134, 135
Luxembourg museum • 30

M

macaron • 90–93, 135, 136
Madeleine, La • 59, 81, 83
Maïolino, Fabien • 85, 86
mairie • 23, 71
Maison des Trois Thés, La • 84, 85–86, 135
Maison du Chocolat, La • 89
Maison du Miel, La • 81
Maison Kayser • 92
Malitourne, J. Y. • 92, 93
Mansart, François • 62
Mara des bois • 87, 88, 135
Marais • 20, 83, 84
Marchal, Gilles • 89
Marcolini, Pierre • 14
Margeon, Gérard • 15
Mariage Frères • 83–84, 86
Marie-Thérèse • 91
Matisse • 6, 7, 134
Matisse, Henri • 43
meerkat • 11, 134
Melchisedech • 68
Mesnager, Jerôme • 10
Mignard, Pierre • 60, 65, 135
Miller, Lee • 43
Miss Tic • 9, 11, 134
Mitterand, François • 1
Modigliani, Amedeo • 41
Monnier, Adrienne • 35
Montagne Sainte-Geneviève • 93, 119
Montmartre • 136
Montparnasse • 29, 41–43
Montparnasse cemetery • 40, 42, 135
Morrison, Toni • 117, 136
Mosko et Associés • 11, 134
mosque • 17–18, 134
Mosquée • 17–18, 83
Moulin Rouge • 22
Muscle Man • 10, 134
Musée de la Fraise et du Patrimoine • 88
Muséum National d'Histore Naturelle • 113

N

Nail of the Passion • 53, 54
Napoleon III • 2
National Apiculture Syndicate • 80
National Library • 53
Nazis • 2
Nemo • 10, 11
Nemrod, Le • 19
Nespresso • 102
Nestor, Hieromonk • 53, 54, 55, 135
Nixon, Nicholas • 38
Notre-Dame Cathedral • 25, 52–55, 59, 135
Nuns' Apiary • 79

O

Occupation • 2, 36
Occupation of Paris • 2
Odalisque • 31
Olivier • 7–8, 134
Opéra • 41, 80, 81
Oursin, L' • 99
oysters • 24, 103–104
    Arcachon • 104
    Belon • 104
    Bouzigues • 103
    Fines de Claire • 104

P

Paik, Nam June • 14
pain au chocolat • 19
Palais des Thés, Le • 84, 86
Palais Garnier • 80
Palais-Royal garden • 81, 136
Parc Georges Brassens • 79
Parc Kellerman • 79, 81
Paris and Île de France Adventure Guide • 39
Paris Montparnasse • 43
Paris Plage • 3–4
Paris-by-the-Beach • 3–4, 134
passage de l'Opéra • 41
passage Richelieu • 38, 135
pâtisserie • 19, 89, 91, 92
Pâtissier du Marché • 93

Paucton, Jean • 80
Pegoty • 83, 86
Père Lachaise cemetery • 81
Père Noël • 23
Perronet, Jean-Rodolphe • 2
pétanque • 3, 4
Petlura, Simon • 58
Philip IV • 61
Philippe II Auguste • 71
Picasso, Pablo • 41, 43
Pigalle • 22
Pigalle, Jean-Baptiste • 68
Pingeot, Bruno • 12
place de la Bastille • 80
place de la Concorde • 1, 2, 83
place Edmond Rostand • 95, 96
place Pablo Picasso • 41, 43
place Saint-Michel • 22
place Vendôme • 24
plaque • 57, 59, 69, 135
Plougastel • 88
poissonerie • 49
Pompidou museum • 20
Pont Alexandre III • 134
Pont au Change • 3
Pont des Arts • 3
Pont Neuf • 3, 6
Pound, Ezra • 29, 36
Prin, Alice • 41
Prussians • 2
Publicis Drugstore • *See* Drugstore Publicis
pyramid • 33, 37, 38, 135
pyramid, inverted • 37, 38, 135

Q

Quatre Parties du Monde, Les • 136
Quintinie, La • 87

R

Radnitsky, Emmanuel • 41
Raft of the Medusa • 117
Ray, Juliet • 40, 42, 135
Ray, Man • 41–43, 135

Ray, Man and Juliet • 40, 135
Rayographs • 42
regent of France • 61
religious orders • 61
  Capucins • 61
  Feuillantines • 61
  Ursulines • 61
Rembrandt • *See* van Rijn, Rembrandt
reveillon • 24, 103
Richelieu • 61
Richelieu wing • 33, 135
Rita • 5–6, 8, 134
Robert the Pious • 71, 72
Rocher de Cancale, Au • 20
Rond-Point • 2
rood screen • 57, 64, 71
Rostand, Le • 95, 96
Roth, Daniel • 69
Rotonde, La • 40, 41, 135
Rousset, Pierre-Noël • 73
Royal Abbey of Val-de-Grâce • 61
Rucher aux Sœurs • 79
Rucher de France, Au • 81
rue Berger • 111
rue Campagne Première • 42
rue Daru • 55
rue Daubenton • 17
rue de Bourbon le Château • 49
rue de l'Amiral de Coligny • 71
rue de l'Estrapade • 99
rue de Lille • 57
rue de l'Odéon • 35, 135
rue de Naples • 81
rue de Rivoli • 96
rue de Rome • 81
rue de Seine • 49
rue de Valence • 99
rue Delambre • 42
rue des Carmes • 57
rue des Ecoles • 57
rue des Martyrs • 22
rue des Saints-Pères • 58

rue Descartes • 119

rue du Bourg-Tibourg • 20, 83, 86

rue du Cherche-Midi • 19

rue du Faubourg Saint-Honoré • 1, 2, 24

rue du Pont-de-Lodi • 83

rue du Puits-de-l'Ermite • 18

rue du Val-de-Grâce • 62

rue Dupuytren • 35

rue Galande • 22, 119

rue Geoffroy Saint-Hilaire • 17, 18, 83, 136

rue Gracieuse • 85, 86

rue Montorgueil • 20

rue Mouffetard • 7, 93, 100, 119

rue Perrault • 73

rue Racine • 58

rue Royale • 83

rue Saint-Denis • 111

rue Saint-Honoré • 24, 64, 96

rue Verlet • 14

rue Vielle du Temple • 84, 86

rue Vignon • 81

S

Sacré-Cœur Basilica • 1, 37

Saee, Michele • 12, 13

Saint Anne • 64

Saint Anthony of the Fifteen-Twenties • 58

Saint Bartholomew's Day Massacre • 72

Saint Denis • 72

Saint Elizabeth • 64

Saint Ephrem the Syrian • 57

Saint Genevieve • 72

Saint Joachim • 64

Saint John the Baptist • 68

Saint Joseph • 64

Saint Mary of Egypt • 72, 135

Saint Michel • 22, 68

Saint Nicolas • 23

Saint Peter • 68

Saint-Alexandre-Nevski Cathedral • 53, 54, 55, 135

Saint-Antoine des Quinze-Vingts • 58

Saint-Antoine-le-Grand • 59

Saint-Cloud • 79

Sainte-Chapelle • 53, 73

Sainte-Geneviève • 57, 93, 119

Saint-Ephrem • 57

Saint-Germain fair • 99

Saint-Germain-des-Prés • 45, 58

Saint-Germain-l'Auxerrois • 70–73, 135

Saint-Julien-le-Pauvre • 119

Saint-Roch church • 64

Saint-Sulpice • 37, 59, 66–69, 135

Saint Vincent • 71

Saint-Vladimir-le-Grand • 58

Saint Zachary • 64

salon de thé • 96

Salon des Copistes du Louvre • 31, 33

Sánchez, Juan • 44–46, 135

Santa Claus • 23

sapin de Noël • 23

Schokmundés, Jean-Jacques • 81

Seine • 4, 6, 9, 136

Shadow Man • 10, 11, 134

Shakespeare and Company • 30, 35

Shu Uemura • 15

smoked salmon • 24

smoking • 15, 48, 49, 78, 85, 95, 96, 97

Société Centrale d'Apiculture • 79

Soulard, Alain • 14

Soutine, Chaim • 42

Speedy Graphito • 134

Starbucks • 6, 102

Starfish • 42

Statue of Liberty • 134

Stein, Gertrude • 29, 43

strawberries • 87–89

Strawberry and Heritage Museum • 88

street sign • 118, 119, 136

Sue, Eugène • 20

Surrealism • 42

Sylvia Beach and the Lost Generation • 36

Syndicat National d'Apiculture • 80, 81

T

Tch'a • 83

tea • 13, 14, 17, 18, 48, 83–86, 91, 95, 99, 135

terroir • 47, 105

Terror, The • 115

Tomb of the Unknown Soldier • 2

torréfacteur • 99, 102

Tour de France • 2

Trotsky, Leon • 41

Tseng, Yu Hui • 85

Tuileries garden • 1, 37, 96, 134, 136

turkey • 25, 103, 104

Tzara, Tristan • 42

U

Uemura, Shu • *See* Shu Uemura

Ulysses • 36

V

Val-de-Grâce • 61–65, 135

Valentine's Day • 95

van Rijn, Rembrandt • 33

Vélasquez, Diego • 33

Vélib' • 108–109, 136

Veneration of the Crown of Thorns • 53

Versailles • 87

Viaduc des Arts • 58

Viollet-le-Duc, Eugène • 72

Violon d'Ingres, Le • 42

Virgin Mary • 64

W

wild game • 25, 104

windmill • 22, 136

wine • 12, 13, 15, 22, 44, 45–47, 77, 84, 86,
    103–105, 134, 135
    Aloxe-Corton • 104
    Bandol • 104
    Banyuls • 105
    Beaune • 104
    Chablis • 14, 104
    Chambertin • 104
    Corton • 104

Corton Charlemagne • 104

Coteaux du Layon • 103

Côte-Rôtie • 104, 136

Côtes de Beaune • 104

Côtes de Nuits • 104

Côtes du Rhone • 104, 136

Ermitage • 104

Graves • 104

Gros Plant • 104

Maury • 105

Meursault • 104

Montrachet • 104

Muscadet • 104

Nuits Saint-Georges • 104

Picpoul de Pinet • 104

Pinot Noir • 103

Pomerol • 104

Porto • 105

Rivesaltes • 105

Romanée • 104

Saint-Emilion • 104

Sancerre • 105

Sauternes • 103, 105

Savigny les Beaune • 104

vin jaune • 105

vins doux naturels • 105

Vouvray • 103

Yquem • 105

wine *cave* • 12, 134

World War I • 2, 17, 41

World War II • 2, 88

Y

Yule log • 103

Yvelines, Les • 9

Photos and Credits

Discover Paris!™ wishes to thank those named in the illustration captions for supplying the photographs included in this publication. Unless otherwise mentioned in captions or below, photographs were contributed by Discover Paris!™

Front cover: Candelabra, Pont Alexandre III
Page xiii: Tom Reeves ©**Diana Lui**
Page xiv: Café de la Mairie Terrace—Paris 6e *arrondissement*
Page xvi: Upper left— Grande Arche de la Défense
Middle left—Tuileries Garden
Lower left—Children's Potager, Tuileries Garden
Upper right— Ferris wheel
Lower right— Champs-Elysées
Page 4: Paris-by-the-Beach
Page 6: Top to bottom—Rita, Matisse, and Jimpy
Page 8: Olivier and Jimpy
Page 10: Top to bottom—Miss Tic—"Poetry is a sport of the extreme."
Speedy Graphito, Muscle Man and Shadow Man Gymnastics
Page 11: Top to Bottom right—Muscle Man at an Irish Pub, Meerkat, Shadow Man and Hippo, Mosko et Associés Rainbow,
Bottom left: Muscle Man reaching
Page 12: Top to bottom—Publicis Drugstore bar, brasserie, press stand, and wine *cave*.
All photos courtesy of **publicisdrugstore**.
Page 14: Drugstore façade
Page 16: Upper—Mosque minaret
Lower—Entry to courtyard
Page 18: Mosque courtyard
Page 21: Upper— Feria Café
Lower—Indiana Bar at Bastille
Page 24: Left—Champagne for Christmas
Right—Boutique Clair de Rêve at Christmas, Ile Saint-Louis
Page 26: Statue of Liberty, Luxembourg Garden
Page 28: La Closerie des Lilas
Page 32: Top to bottom—Phase 1, Phase 2, and Phase 3 of copying *La Baigneuse* at the Louvre.
All photos courtesy of **Jane**.

Page 33:   Louvre—Richelieu wing and pyramid

Page 34:   Plaque at 12, rue de l'Odéon, Paris 6e *arrondissement*

Page 38:   Top—Pyramid viewed from Passage Richelieu

Bottom—Inverted pyramid

Page 40:   Top—La Rotonde

Middle—Man and Juliet Ray—Photo from tombstone at
Montparnasse cemetery

Bottom—Le Dôme

Page 44:   Top to bottom—Juan Sánchez, La Dernière Goutte façade, Wine
stock

Page 50:   Val-de-Grâce

Page 52:   Notre-Dame Cathedral

Page 54:   Saint-Alexandre-Nevski Cathedral

Page 55:   Hieromonk Nestor

Page 56:   Eglise Saint-Antoine des Quinze-Vingts

Page 58:   Eglise Saint-Ephrem

Page 60:   Cupola fresco by Pierre Mignard, Val-de-Grâce

Page 62:   Cupola of Val-de-Grâce

Page 63:   Nave

Page 64:   Marble floor at Val-de-Grâce

Page 66:   Organ at Saint-Sulpice

Page 70:   Eglise Saint-Germain-l'Auxerrois

Page 73:   Sculpture of the façade of Eglise Saint-Germain-l'Auxerrois

Top—Saint Mary of Egypt

Middle—Dragon

Bottom—Human

Page 74:   Fresh breads and pastries

Page 76:   Clockwise from upper left— Finishing a dish at La Bastide Odéon,
Asparagus risotto, Dining room at La Table d'Erica, Dining room at
Chez Lena et Mimile

Photo of La Bastide Odéon courtesy of **Apicius**.

Page 80:   Luxembourg Garden apiary

Page 82:   Japanese tea ceremony

Page 84:   Upper—La Maison des Trois Thés

Lower—Weighing tea

Page 88:   Left—Gariguettes

Right—Mara des Bois

Page 90:   *Macaron*-festooned cakes

Page 92:   Top—Colorful *macarons*

Middle—*Pièce montée* at Ladurée

Bottom—Pierre Hermé *macarons*

Page 94:   Hot chocolate at La Charlotte de l'Isle

Page 98:   Jean-Paul Logereau

Page 101:   Upper—Fresh-roasted coffee

Lower—Sampling the roast

Page 104:   Côtes du Rhone—Côte-Rôtie

Page 105:   Champagne and *chou* pastry

Page 106:   Scenes from Montmartre

Upper left—Eglise Saint-Jean-l'Evangéliste

Lower left—Windmill

Upper right— Preparing lavender bouquets

Middle right—Carrousel at the base of Montmartre hill

Lower right—Montmartre train

Page 108:   *Vélib'* station

Page 110:   La Fontaine des Innocents

Page 112:   Scenes from the Jardin des Plantes

Clockwise from left: Entry at rue Geoffroy Saint-Hilaire, Flower bed, Menagerie, Iron gazebo

Page 113:   Dragon

Page 114:   Guillotine

Page 116:   Toni Morrison at the Louvre

Page 118:   Oldest street sign in Paris

Page 119:   Left—Eglise Saint-Julien-le-Pauvre

Right—Roman paving stone

Page 120:   Pol Bury fountain at the Palais-Royal garden

Page 122:   Eiffel Tower and stepped gardens

Page 124:   Sunset viewed from the Seine

Back cover: Left to right—Sailboats at the Tuileries garden; *Les Quatre Parties du Monde* by Jean-Baptiste Carpeaux; Arc de Triomphe—Bastille Day décor

CPSIA information can be obtained at www.ICGtesting.com
Printed in the USA
BVOW060844200912

300839BV00003B/24/P

9 780981 529240